Poetry Through Humour and Horror

Chris Webster

CASSELL

To Julie

I would like to acknowledge, with grateful thanks, all the pupils with whom I have shared an enjoyment of poetry, particularly those at Appleton School, South Benfleet, who contributed so enthusiastically to the making of this book.

I would also like to thank Margaret Scorthorne for her hard work typing the manuscript.

Cassell Educational Limited
Artillery House
Artillery Row
London SW1P 1RT

British Library Cataloguing in Publication Data
Poetry through humour and horror.
  1. Children's poetry, English
  I. Webster, Chris
  821'.008   PR1175.3

ISBN: 0–304–31354–8

Typeset by Columns Ltd
Designed by Lesley Stewart
Printed and bound in Great Britain by Billing and Son Ltd.

Last digit is print no: 9 8 7 6 5 4 3 2 1

Contents

Acknowledgements

The publishers and author would like to thank all those who have permitted the use of copyright material in their books. Sources are as follows: Anonymous – 'Once there was a man', 'What is frozen water?', 'Will you remember me', knock-knock jokes, 'A little girl', 'Teacher', *The Crack a Joke Book*, Puffin Books; 'Horrible sandwich fillings', 'Nobody loves me', *The End*, ed. R. Stanley, Puffin Books; 'Nine herbs charm', 'Journey spell', *Anglo-Saxon Poetry*, Everyman Books; 'Rain magic song', *The Penguin Book of Oral Poetry*, Penguin Books; 'Rhyme puzzle', 'There were three ghostesses', 'The ankle', *The Beaver Book of Funny Rhymes*, ed. B. Ireson, Arrow Books; 'A skeleton', 'There was a young girl', 'There was a young lady', *The Penguin Book of Limericks*, Penguin Books; 'There was a young man', *The Art of the Limerick*, C. Bibby, Fudge & Co. Ltd; 'The demon lover' derived from *Border Ballads*, Walter Scott Publishing Co.; 'Miss Ellen Gee', 'One old Oxford ox', 'Marezle toats', *The Faber Book of Nonsense Verse*, ed. G. Grigson, Faber & Faber; 'Hinx minx', *The Beaver Book of Creepy Verse*, eds I. and Z. Woodward, Arrow Books; 'Belagcholly days', *A Choice of Comic and Curious Verse*, ed. J.H. Cohen, Penguin Books; 'Stately verse', *The Puffin Book of Funny Verse*, ed. J. Watson, Puffin Books; 'Things you never saw', *Puffin Joke Book*, Puffin Books; 'Prophecies of Mother Shipton', *The Life and Prophecies of Ursula Sonthiel*, S. Maclean, Arthur Wigley & Sons; 'Charm', 'Song of two ghosts', 'Song of expiation', 'Thief's spell', 'Ombrure calls up the forest spirits', 'Blackened-face', 'Song of the animal world', *The Unwritten Songs*, ed. W.R. Trask, Macmillan (New York). Douglas Adams 'Vogon poetry', *The Hitchhiker's Guide to the Galaxy*, Pan Books; J. Berry 'Dialogue between two large village women', *Caribbean Poetry Now*, ed. S. Brown, Hodder & Stoughton Educational; R. Blair 'Church and churchyard at night' (modernised), *The Oxford Book of Eighteenth Century Verse*, ed. D. Nichol Smith, Oxford University Press; William Blake 'The silk rose', *The Illuminated Blake*, ed. D. Eerdman, Harvard College Library; F. Bodmer 'Japanese characters', *The Loom of Language*, George Allen & Unwin Ltd; Emily Bronte 'Spellbound', *The New Oxford Book of English Verse*, Oxford University Press; Lewis Carroll 'Acrostic', 'Double acrostic', 'Lorenzo dwelt at Heighington', *Lewis Carroll: The Complete Works*, Nonesuch Press; Jasper Carrott 'Mystical musings of a contented till', *Sweet and Sour Labrador*, Arrow Books; G.K. Chesterton 'When fishes flew', *Rhyme and Rhythm*, eds J. Gibson and R. Wilson, Macmillan; John Cleese et al., 'First draft', *The Brand New Monty Python Bok*, Methuen, London; 'Clerihews', 'Radi', *Versicles and Limericks*, ed. C. Connell, Beaver Books; e.e. cummings 'Hist whist', *Complete Poems 1913–1962*, Grafton Books; Walter de la Mare 'The feckless dinner party', *Georgian Poetry*, ed. G. Reeves, Heinemann © Society of Authors; Dinka (trad.) 'The magnificent bull', Deepak Kalha 'Fear', H.O. Nazareth 'Reasons for extinction', *I Like That Stuff*, ed. M. Styles,

Cambridge University Press; Roy Fuller 'Be a monster', *Poor Roy*, Andre Deutsch Ltd © Roy Fuller; Alan Garner 'Albanac's spell', *The Moon of Gomrath*, Armada Lion; Nicolás Guillén 'Sensemaya: a chant for killing a snake', *New Ships: an Anthology of West Indian Poems*, ed. D.G. Wilson, Oxford University Press © Mrs Helen Coulthard; Ted Hughes 'Nessie', *Moon-Bells and Other Poems*, Chatto & Windus © 1979, 1986 Ted Hughes, reprinted by permission of Olwyn Hughes; Igbo (trad.) 'You', *Poetic Heritage: Igbo Traditional Verse*, ed. Egudu and Nwoga, Heinemann Educational; Edward Lear 'Limerick', *The Art of the Limerick*, C. Bibby, Fudge & Co. Ltd; 'Riddles', 'Letter to Evelyn', *The Faber Book of Nonsense Verse*, ed. G. Grigson, Faber & Faber; Brian Lee 'All on my own', 'The queer moment', *Late Home*, Kestrel Books © 1986 Brian Lee; Roger McGough 'First day at school', 'Autumn poem', *In the Glassroom*, Jonathan Cape Ltd, 'Blood is an acquired taste' *Gig*, Jonathan Cape Ltd, 'Gruesome', *You Tell Me*, Kestrel Books, reprinted by permission of A.D. Peters & Co. Ltd; William Mayne 'Haunted', *Hist Whist*, ed. D. Saunders and K. Wyatt, Hamish Hamilton; Harold Munro 'Overheard on a saltmarsh', *Georgian Poetry*, ed. G. Reeves, Heinemann; Spike Milligan 'The ABC', *Silly Verse for Kids*, Puffin Books, 'A goblin funeral director', *Goblins*, Arrow Books, 'Terence newt' *The Bedside Milligan*, Tandem Books; Christian Morgenstern and Man Ray 'Phonetic poems', *Dada*, H. Richter, Thames & Hudson; Ogden Nash 'Away from it all', *Many Long Years Ago* (1954), Andre Deutsch Ltd; Alma Norman 'The curse of Rose Hall', *New Ships: An Anthology of West Indian Poetry*, ed. D.G. Wilson, Oxford University Press © Alma Norman; Mervyn Peake 'Little spider', 'O'er seas that have no beaches', 'O here it is', *A Book of Nonsense*, Peter Owen; Jack Prelutsky 'Wild witches' ball', 'The haunted house', *Nightmares: Poems to Trouble Your Sleep*, A & C Black Ltd; Pygmy (trad.) 'Song of the animal world', *Rhymes and Rhythms*, ed. D. Woolger, Oxford University Press; Seamus Redmond 'The silent spinney', *The Beaver Book of Creepy Verse*, ed. I. and Z. Woodward, Arrow Books; James Reeves 'Moths and moonshine', *The Complete Poems for Children*, Heinemann © James Reeves Estate; M. Rosen 'I'm just going out for a moment', Shen Silverstein 'I am writing these lines' and Peter Wesley Smith 'Chuffa-luffa steam train', *The Beaver Book of Funny Rhymes*, ed. B. Ireson, Arrow Books; Ian Serrallier 'Riddle', *The Beaver Book of Creepy Verse*, ed. I. and Z. Woodward, Arrow Books; Rabindranath Tagore 'The last tryst' (extract), *Selected Poems*, translated by William Radice, Penguin Books © 1985 William Radice; Carolyn Wells 'A tutor who . .', *The Puffin Book of Funny Verse*, ed. J. Watson, Puffin Books.

Every effort has been made to trace the copyright holders of the material reproduced in this book. Where this has not been possible we apologise to those concerned.

Introduction

TO THE TEACHER

The companion teachers' book contains an introduction for teachers, detailed advice on how to use this book, a chapter by chapter guide, and suggestions for follow-up work and further reading. It is available from the publishers, free on request.

TO THE PUPIL

The aim of this book is to convince you that poetry can be just as exciting as the late night horror film—more so because you can create it yourself! In these pages you will find witches, haunted houses, vampires and many other horrors to enjoy reading about, and give you lots of ideas for writing.

If the horror doesn't get you interested, perhaps the humour will. You will have so much fun with the limericks, nonsense poems and the tantalisingly tricky tongue-twisters, that next time you feel like a good laugh you will be more likely to reach for a poetry book than a joke book!

You will also find puzzles and riddles to test your skill, challenging questions to get you thinking and talking, and a host of horrific and humorous poems by famous poets (and not-so-famous pupils like yourselves) to inspire you to write poems which are even spookier and funnier!

Just a final word of advice. If, one night when you are sitting up late doing your poetry homework, the wind starts to howl and you hear footsteps on the stairs, turn to the nonsense poetry to cheer yourself up, and try not to panic, it's only your mum bringing you a cup of tea—or is it?

Chris Webster
Great Wakering 1986

1
Capturing Ghosts

I thought I saw a ghost last night
I hadn't got my camera
So I described it in free verse
(I hadn't time
To make it rhyme)
It was hooded
With a monkish cowl
And white
White as a sheet—
It even had flowery patterns round the edge
Like those on my brother's bed
So I hit it
And this morning my brother James
Has got a poorly head!

If you had just seen a ghost, writing a poem would be the last thing you would think about! But assuming you had escaped to a safe distance, and you *did* want to write a poem, you would want to write quickly, while the fear was still tingling in your spine. If you spent too much time counting syllables and thumbing through a rhyming dictionary the experience would have gone stale by the time you had finished—the ghost would have escaped! This is true of most ideas for poetry; you have to capture that first inspiration to make a good poem. That's why free verse is used by many modern poets. It allows them to concentrate on what they want to say rather than finding rhymes and fitting metres. Rhyme and metre are only two of the many ingredients that can make up a poem. They are not essential—but they *are* difficult to use, and can easily lead you into saying something that doesn't make sense, which is what happened in this poem:

George the Third
Was a very strange bird.
(He was really a king,
But 'king' wouldn't rhyme with 'third'.)

The advantage of free verse is that it allows you to concentrate on your subject and the best way of expressing it without having to worry about rhyme and other technicalities. Lines can be of any length, even as short as one word, and can be set out in any way that brings out the meaning. The occasional rhyme can be used, providing it occurs naturally and is not part of a preset pattern. In short, you can do what you like—you make the rules—you don't even have to use capital letters or punctuation if you don't want to! So if you see a ghost, and you haven't got your camera handy, try capturing it in free verse! Meanwhile, unless your classroom is haunted, you will have to rely on these examples for inspiration:

The Dark Wood

In the dark, dark, wood
Was a dark, dark house,
In the dark, dark house
Was a dark, dark room,
In the dark, dark room
Was a dark, dark cupboard,
In the dark, dark cupboard
Was a dark, dark shelf,
And on the dark, dark shelf
Was a dark, dark box,
And in that dark, dark box
Was a GHOST!

                    Traditional

Song of Two Ghosts

My friend
This is a wide world
We're travelling over
Walking on the moonlight.

            Omaha Indians,
            North America

Fear

Curling fingers
crawling up
the back
of your
brain,
taking your mind
by
surprise,
then gripping
your heart and
squeezing it
of its
life source.
A plunger
pushing
the contents
of your
stomach
down and
out.

            Deepak Kalha

hist whist

hist whist
little ghostthings
tip-toe
twinkle-toe

little twitchy
witches and tingling
goblins
hob-a-nob hob-a-nob

little hoppy happy
toad in tweeds
tweeds
little itchy mousies

with scuttling
eyes   rustle and run   and
hidehidehide
whisk

whisk   look out for the old woman
with the wart on her nose
what she'll do to yer
nobody knows

for she knows the devil   ooch
the devil   ouch
the devil
ach   the great

green
dancing
devil
devil

devil
devil

wheeEEE

e.e. cummings

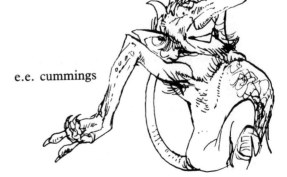

Haunted

Black hill
black hall
all still
owl's grey cry
edges shrill
castle night.

Woken eye
round in fright;
what lurks walks
in castle rustle?

Hand cold
held hand
the moving roving
urging thing;
dreamed margin

voiceless
noiseless
HEARD
feared
a ghost passed

black hill
black hall
all still
owl's grey cry
edges shrill
castle night.

William Mayne

Charm

Whispering ghosts of the west,
Who brought you here
To our land?
Stand up and depart.
Whispering ghosts of the west,
Who brought you here
To our land?
Stand up and depart.

Maori, New Zealand

Footsteps

Slow, heavy footsteps
On the cold, creaky floorboards.
Someone is in the house!

I tiptoed up the stairs
Armed with a heavy saucepan
But I didn't find a vampire,
Spook or apparition,
Just Tiddles trapped in my room!

Zoe Goodall, aged 12

Werewolf

Flea-bitten and shaggy,
Gruesome and vile,
Blood dripping
From his white fangs.

Man one minute,
Wolf the next,
Hiding in the shadows,
Waiting to strike.

Will you be next?

Stephen Boyce, aged 12

Song of Expiation

Spirits of the forest, night-walking ghosts
Who during the bright day,
Like bats that suck men's blood,
Hang hooked to the slippery walls of great caves,
Behind the green moss, behind the great white stones—
Tell us: Who has seen them, the night-walking ghosts?
Tell us: Who has seen them?

Pygmy, Cameroon

Some Rules for Visiting a Deserted House

Look behind the door for letters.
Any that you find read sympathetically.
If there are bills decide to pay them.

Don't worry about rats.
If any colony existed
there will be no survivors.
Rats, too, are cannibals.

As for ghosts
they will not be those of popular fiction
but intermingled and continuous with the air.
You will be all right if you don't stay too long
or breathe too deeply.

Watch out for the loose section of carpet
When going up the stairs.
It will be in a different place
when you come down.

Avoid the mirror on the landing.
It will be thirsty.

Check the bedroom.
If there is only one impression on the pillow
make another.
If there are two, erase one.

Check the bathroom.
If something looks like rust in the bathtub
wet it.
Touch it to see if it feels sticky.

In the loft, under the eaves,
will be the skeletons of small trapped birds.
You may examine them
but be sure to put them back.
They are trophies.

If, in spite of everything,
you find the outside door jammed shut
when you are ready to depart
don't bother going to the windows.
They also will have been attended to.
Sit down and wait.
Try not to think about the small birds.

Alasdair Maclean

DISCUSSION

Which of these poems did you like best? What did you like about it? Which bits were the most frightening? What made them frightening?

'hist whist' shows you how free free verse can be: it doesn't even have commas or full stops. How has the spacing of words and the layout of lines been used instead of punctuation?

Poetry does not have to be written in clear sentences in which everything is fully explained. It is often more effective to use words and short phrases which hint at sounds, sights and feelings, but leave much to the imagination (see how e.e. cummings and William Mayne have done this). Why is this technique particularly effective when writing about ghosts?

Do you think poems should rhyme? Why? Would you have enjoyed these examples more if they had rhymed? What other things make poems different from ordinary writing?

Poets sometimes repeat certain words or lines, or even whole verses. Find and discuss some examples of this. How does it add to the effect of the poem?

Finally, to get you in the mood for writing, take it in turn to tell ghost stories to each other.

WRITING

Think about the ghost poems and stories that you have discussed, close your eyes and imagine that one of them is happening to you.

> What did you hear?
> What did you see?
> How did you feel?
> What happened?

Quickly jot down some words and phrases to describe these things—remember, there is no need to write in complete sentences! Read over what you have written. What improvements can you make? (Resist the temptation to use rhyme.) When you are satisfied, make a neat copy of your poem.

Re-read 'The Dark Wood' and write a poem with a similar pattern. Here's a suggestion to complete:

> In the weird old church
> Was a weird old crypt.
> In the weird old crypt
> Was a ——————
> (etc.)

Re-read the poem that begins the chapter. Who is the ghost in this poem? Write your own poem about a ghost that turned out to be something quite ordinary!

Jot down all the ways you know of killing a vampire, then write a poem entitled 'Some Rules for Hunting Vampires'.

Make a display in poems and pictures of all the ghosts 'captured' by your class.

Poetry Puzzle

Here is a free verse poem written out like prose.

Re-write it, setting it out as poetry.

Begin new lines and verses, and use punctuation as and when you think necessary to bring out the meaning of the poem.

Finally, think of a suitable title for the poem.

> dracula his bright red staring eyes red red like his teeth like my blood i wish he wouldn't look at me like that as though i'm on his menu for tonight wouldn't he prefer some fish and chips with tomato sauce or blood not my blood or a juicy steak i'd much rather he had a steak a steak a stake a stake through the heart but it's too late too late he's having me instead ouch i'm dead no i'm not i'm awake what a rotten nightmare what's this ooch a mosquito bite

Compare your version with a friend's and discuss your reasons for beginning new lines, or verses, or putting in punctuation. Whose version brings out the sense most clearly and is easiest to read?

How can you tell that the passage above is meant to be poetry, even though it is set out as prose?

What is poetry—apart from the obvious features of rhyme, rhythm and layout on the page? (There are no easy answers to this one!)

2
Funny Free Verse

What is frozen water? Ice.
What is frozen cream? Ice cream.
What is frozen tea? Iced tea.
What is frozen ink? Iced ink.
    WELL, HAVE A BATH THEN!

Is this a joke or a poem? The answer is that it is both! It is certainly a joke, and a funny one at that (try it on your friends and see!), but it is also a poem, even though there is no rhyme, because the words are arranged in a pattern.

Below is a selection of other funny free verse poems. Some of them, like the one above, have been taken from joke books; others are from poetry books. Try to guess which is which. Then re-read them more carefully, looking out for patterns made by repeated words and phrases, and for the way in which they have been divided into lines and set out on the page.

Nobody loves me, everybody hates me
I'm going in the garden to eat worms.
Long slim slimy ones,
Short fat fuzzy ones,
Gooey—ooey—ooey ones.
The long slim slimy ones slip down easily,
The short fat fuzzy ones stick to your teeth,
And make you go urr urr yum yum.

                       Anon

Horrible Sandwich Fillings

Custard and sand
Toothpaste and gravel
Raw liver and clay
Sawdust and candle grease
Mousetails and mustard pickle
Ashes and ice-cream
Hamster bedding and vegetable oil
Nuts, shells and ink
Mouldy leaves and rats' ears
Chalk dust and tree sap
Squashed worms and washing-up liquid
Dog food and bird seed
Mushy banana and cement

Anon

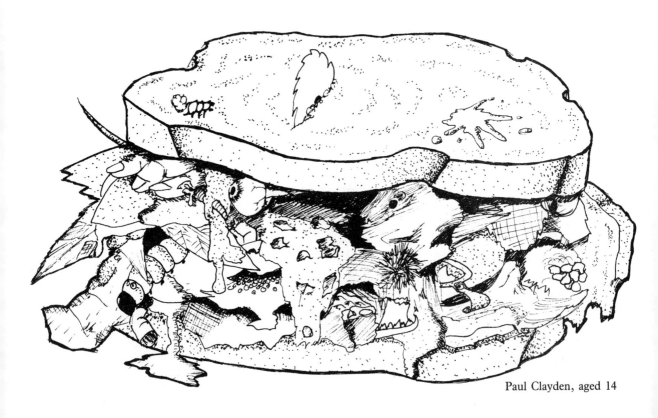

Paul Clayden, aged 14

You!

You!
Your head is like a drum that is beaten for spirits.
You!
Your ears are like the fans used for blowing fires.
You!
Your nostril is like a mouse's den.
You!
Your mouth is like a mound of mud.
You!
Your hands are like drum-sticks.
You!
Your belly is like a pot of rotten water.
You!
Your legs are like stakes.
You!
Your buttocks are like a mountain top.

Traditional Igbo

You!

Your hair is like a toupee bought from a pedlar.
You!
Your face looks like your buttocks in the wrong place.
You!
Your nose! Your nose looks like Concorde's rear end.
You!
Your eyes are like a manky cat's in the dark.
You!
Your ears are like cauliflower—all soggy and split.
You!
Your trousers, your trousers, look at those trousers all baggy and ripped.
You!
Your belt, your belt is like a python's weird tongue.
You!
Your feet are like lumps of cheese.
But you,
You're not bad!

Bryan Smith, aged 11

Once there was a man who wouldn't stop singing. He was told that if he didn't keep quiet, he would be put in front of the firing squad, but he still carried on.
Preparations were made for his execution. Before the soldiers aimed, the man asked if, as his last wish, he might sing a song. This was granted and he began to sing a song entitled '10 000 Green Bottles'.

Anon

Dialogue Between Two Large Village Women

Vergie mi gal, yu know
wha overtek me?

    Wha, Bet-Bet darlin?

Yu know de downgrow bwoy
dey call Runt?

    Everybody know de lickle
    forceripe wretch.

Well mi dear, de bwoy put
question to mi.

    Wha? Wha yu sey?

Yeahs—put question to mi
big-big woman, who could be
him mummah over and over.

    Laad above. Didn yu bounce
    de damn lickle ramgoat face?

Mi hol him an mi shake
de lickle beas like
to kill de wretch.
An yu know wha happn?

    No.

De lickle brute try fi kiss mi.

James Berry

I'm Just Going Out for a Moment

I'm just going out for a moment.
Why?
To make a cup of tea.
Why?
Because I'm thirsty.
Why?
Because it's hot.
Why?
Because the sun's shining.
Why?
Because it's summer.
Why?
Because that's when it is.
Why?
Why don't you stop saying why?
Why?

Mike Rosen

Will you remember me in a month?
  Of course!
Will you remember me in a year?
  Certainly.
Will you remember me in two years?
  Yes.
Will you remember me in three years?
  Of course!
Knock, knock.
  Who's there?
See, you've forgotten me already.

Anon

First Day at School

A millionbillionwillion miles from home
Waiting for the bell to go. (To go where?)
Why are they all so big, other children?
So noisy? So much at home they
must have been born in uniform.
Lived all their lives in playgrounds.
Spent the years inventing games
that don't let me in. Games
that are rough, that swallow you up.

And the railings.
All around, the railings.
Are they to keep out wolves and monsters?
Things that carry off and eat children?
Things you don't take sweets from?
Perhaps they're to stop us getting out.
Running away from the lessins. Lessin.
What does a lessin look like?
Sounds small and slimy.
They keep them in glassrooms.
Whole rooms made out of glass. Imagine.

I wish I could remember my name.
Mummy said it would come in useful.
Like wellies. When there's puddles.
Yellowwellies. I wish she was here.
I think my name is sewn on somewhere.
Perhaps the teacher will read it for me.
Tea-cher. The one who makes the tea.

Roger McGough

Mystical Musings of a Contented Till or I £CHING!

I've never really understood
why people who
write poetry like
this
get paid a
bob
or two
surely it's not difficult to write
it
in fact I just have
haven't I
oh no
you must put lots
of words in
like
memory
tomorrow
misty
nebulous
ethereal that's a good one
phew it's ever such hard work
honest
right then
now
where's my
money?

Jasper Carrott

School

School is like a rubbish dump
with writing on the desks,
all the cupboards are off their hinges
and the chairs are half collapsed.
Cold floors, old dusty black-boards
which really aren't that black.
Working is a punishment for something
we didn't do,
and we wish we didn't go there
'cause it smells a lot too.

Louise Appleby, aged 11

DISCUSSION

Which of these poems was the funniest? What was it that made you laugh?

Can you tell which of these poems were taken from joke books, and which were taken from poetry books? How?

One of these examples is not a poem at all: it is written in prose (prose is ordinary writing—these questions are written in prose). Which one is it? How could you tell? What changes would you have to make to set it out like a poem?

In 'Dialogue Between Two Large Village Women' dialect has been used to add to the humour. What dialect is it? What different dialects are there in your class?

In 'First Day at School' Roger McGough plays with the sound and sense of words. Find some examples of this and explain how they work. What does Jasper Carrott think of poets who write free verse? Do you agree with him?

WRITING

Copy out 'Horrible Sandwich Fillings' and add some more lines of your own. Write a poem entitled 'A Disgusting Recipe'. Compile a class booklet or display of disgusting recipes complete with illustrations.

Try doing what Bryan Smith did and write an insult poem using the same pattern as 'You' (but don't name names, or aim it at anyone in your class—you might end up with a thick ear!).

Write a humorous dialect poem.

Write a poem similar to 'I'm Just Going Out for a Moment'. You might start with one of those things adults often say, such as 'I told you not to eat sweets between meals' or 'Don't speak until you're spoken to'.

Look again at the school poems by Roger McGough (famous poet) and Louise Appleby (first year pupil). Write your own poem about school, ensuring that you take care with your spelling.

Make a collection of jokes in which the words form a pattern.

If you know which of the above examples is written in prose try re-writing it in poetry. Alter and re-arrange the lines as much as you wish (remember how you solved the poetry puzzle on page 8).

Now take any joke you know—preferably one that is longer than just a few lines—and re-shape it into a funny free verse poem.

GROUP POEMS

Work in groups of about four pupils. Begin on your own by adding a line or two to the given line, then combine your lines with everyone else's to make the best possible version of the poem. Pay particular attention to the ending—try to build up to a climax of humour or surprise. The following example was based on the line 'I didn't hand my homework in because . . . .' Note how the pupils edited their lines to create a gradual build-up from simple, everyday excuses to longer and more far-fetched ones.

Excuses

I didn't hand my homework in because
  I forgot it
I didn't hand my homework in because
  I thought I had to hand it in tomorrow
I didn't hand my homework in because
  It blew away on the way to school
I didn't hand my homework in because
  My dog chewed it up
I didn't hand my homework in because
  My mum couldn't do it
I didn't hand my homework in because
  I used all the pages to write love letters
  to a tasty bird round the corner
I didn't hand my homework in because
  I put it in the oven instead of my steak
I didn't hand my homework in because
  I ran out of toilet paper and . . . .
I didn't hand my homework in because
  The *Times Educational Supplement*
  wanted to see it first
I didn't hand my homework in because
  You never mark it anyway
I didn't hand my homework in because
  I tripped over a blade of grass
  the book went hurtling through the air
  into a lady's house
  and hit her on the head
  so she tore it up
  and ate it . . .
     . . . honest

Jamie Hutchins,
Sally Kelleher,
Stephen Oxley,
Grant Smith,
Nina Stafford,
second year pupils

16

Here are some opening lines:

I was late for school because . . .
The funniest thing I ever saw was . . .
School dinners remind me of . . .
(Don't let your dinner ladies see this poem!)
When the bell goes . . .

Poetry Puzzle

Autumn Poem

litter
    is
      turning
        brown
          and
            the
              road
                above
              is
            filled
          with
        hitch
      hikers
    heading
south

                      Roger McGough

What is the 'road above' and who are the hitch-hikers?

How does the layout of the poem give you a clue to the answer?

What other clue is there?

Try writing your own free verse poem in which the layout of the words
helps the meaning.

3
Spells

Have you ever nagged your parents for something for so long that they finally gave in? If you have you'll have an idea of one of the ways spells were thought to work—persuading a god or spirit to grant requests by repeating them over and over again. These days we take a more matter-of-fact view of the world. We know, for example, that if we want a safe journey we must make sensible preparations, such as checking the brakes and lights of a car—we would be unlikely to rely on a spell like this one:

> I guard myself with this rod
> And give myself into God's protection,
>> Against the painful stroke,
>> Against the grievous stroke,
>> Against the grim dread,
>> Against the great terror,
>> And against all evil.
> I grant a charm of victory,
> I bear a rod of victory,
> Word-victory,
> Work-victory.
> May they be of power for me,
> I pray now to the God of victory
> For a good journey.

> Anglo-Saxon

The user of this spell a thousand years ago would have valued it for its protective power rather than its poetry. Yet poetry it is, because words have been used in the same way as in a poem: they have been arranged into a pattern. In these spells it is a pattern of repeated words and phrases. Many other patterns are possible, such as those created by rhyme, rhythm, or the sounds of letters, and these will be explored in later chapters.

As you read the following spells listen for the patterns set by repetition, and note how repeated words and phrases have been used to create a build-up of power.

Thief's Spell

Black concealment be about me!
Black night be about me!
May it be like black soot all about!
Let none be able to see!
Let none be able to see me and recognise me!
Let me be a leguan-lizard, that vanishes unseen!
Let me be a ghost that no one sees!
If the noise I make must be heard,
Let me remain concealed!
Let me be like a ghost,
The sound it makes is heard,
But it is not seen!

> From the Gazelle Peninsula, New Britain

Ombrure Calls up the Forest Spirits

You who rule the forests, spirits of the forests,
All you who obey me, it is I who call you.
Come, come, to the call of your chief.
Answer without lingering, answer now.
I will send the Lightning that passes and splits the sky.
I will send the Thunder that shatters everything.
I will send the Storm Wind that rips the banana trees.
I will send the Rainstorm that drops from the clouds and sweeps everything before it.
All must answer the voice of their chief.

All you who obey me, show me the road,
The road taken by those who have run away.
Spirits of the forest, answer . . .

You who rule the forests, spirits of the forests,
All you who obey me, it is I who call.
Where are men, have they gone by your roads?

> From the Fang *Legend of Ngurangurane*, West Africa

Nine Herbs Charm

Mugwort, plantain which is open eastward, lamb's cress, cock's-spur grass,
mayweed, nettle, crab-apple, thyme and fennel, old soap; crush the herbs to dust,
mix with the soap and with the apple's juice. Make a paste of water and of ashes;
take fennel, boil it in the paste and bathe with egg-mixture, either before or after he
puts on the salve. Sing that charm on each of the herbs; thrice before he works them
together and on the apple likewise; and sing that same charm into the man's mouth
and into both his ears and into the wound before he puts on the salve.

It stands against pain, resists the venom,
It has power against three and against thirty,
Against a fiend's hand and against sudden trick,
Against witchcraft of vile creatures.

Now these nine herbs avail against nine evil spirits,
Against nine poisons and against nine infectious diseases,
Against the red poison, against the running poison,
Against the white poison, against the blue poison,
Against the yellow poison, against the green poison,
Against the black poison, against the blue poison,
Against the brown poison, against the crimson poison,
Against snake-blister, against water-blister,
Against thorn-blister, against thistle-blister,
Against ice-blister, against poison-blister;
If any poison comes flying from the east or any comes from the north,
Or any from the west upon the people.

Christ stood over disease of every kind.
I alone know running water, and the nine serpents heed it;
May all pastures now spring up with herbs,
The seas, all salt water, be destroyed,
When I blow this poison from thee.

Anglo-Saxon

Rain Magic Song

Ready we stand in San Juan town,
O, our Corn Maidens and our Corn Youths!
O, our Corn Mothers and our Corn Fathers!
Now we bring you misty water
And throw it different ways,
To the north, the west, the south, the east
To heaven above and the drinking earth below!
Then likewise throw you misty water
Towards San Juan!
O, many that you are, pour water
Over our Corn Maidens' ears!
On our Wheat Maidens
Thence throw you misty water,
All round about us here!
On Green Earth Woman's back
Now thrives our flesh and breath,
Now grows our strength of arm and leg,
Now takes form our children's food.

Pueblo

Julie Braithwaite, aged 15

All these are genuine spells which have been used at some time or other for magical purposes! Spells are still being written, but now they are usually intended to be enjoyed as poems, such as 'A Chant for Killing a Snake', or as part of a story, such as 'Albanac's Spell' from the novel *The Moon of Gomrath*.

Sensemaya:
A Chant for Killing a Snake

Mayombe-bombe-mayombé!
Mayombe-bombe-mayombé!
Mayombe-bombe-mayombé!

The snake has eyes of glass;
the snake comes and coils itself round a pole;
with his eyes of glass, round a pole,
with his eyes of glass.

The snake walks without legs;
the snake hides in the grass;
walking he hides in the grass
walking without legs.

Mayombe-bombe-mayombé!
Mayombe-bombe-mayombé!
Mayombe-bombe-mayombé!

If you hit him with an axe he will die.
Hit him hard!
Do not hit him with your foot, he will bite,
do not hit him with your foot, he is going away!

Sensemayá, the snake.
Sensemayá,
Sensemayá, with his eyes,
Sensemayá.
Sensemayá, with his tongue,
Sensemayá.
Sensemayá, with his mouth,
Sensemayá.

Dead snake cannot eat;
dead snake cannot hiss;
cannot walk
cannot run.
Dead snake cannot look;
dead snake cannot drink,
cannot breathe,
cannot bite.

Mayombe-bombe-mayombé!
Sensemayá, the snake—
Mayombe-bombe-mayombé!
Sensemayá, it is still—
Mayombe-bombe-mayombé!
Sensemayá, the snake—
Mayombe-bombe-mayombé!
Sensemayá, it is dead.

Nicolás Guillén
Translated by G.R. Coulthard

22

Albanac's Spell
(Spoken by the wizard Albanac to protect Colin and Susan from an evil being called the Brollachan.)

Power of wind have I over thee.
Power of wrath have I over thee.
Power of fire have I over thee.
Power of thunder have I over thee.
Power of lightning have I over thee.
Power of storms have I over thee.
Power of moon have I over thee.
Power of sun have I over thee.
Power of stars have I over thee.
Power of the—heavens—and—of the worlds—have I—over—thee.
Power—power—I cannot hold it!
   Eson! Eson! Emaris!

Alan Garner

Birthday Spell

Tumata-kuru tarata
I want a bike for my birthday
A racer
With drop-handlebars
And a lightweight frame.
Tumata-kuru tarata
I want a bike for my birthday.
Please mum, I'll be a good boy
Please dad, I'll help you wash the car
And I'll try harder at school.
Tumata-kuru tarata
I want a bike for my birthday.

Jozef Jaszkiewicz, aged 12

DISCUSSION

Why were spells important to people of long ago, and still are in some underdeveloped countries today?

What might we do today to ensure a safe journey, and the fertility of the land, or to cure someone who had been poisoned?

Read Albanac's spell again, and discuss what happens at the end of it. To see if you are right, read Chapter Five of *The Moon of Gomrath*.

Discuss the things you wish you had spells for.

WRITING

(Remember that, for the time being, it is better not to use rhyme, but to rely on pattern: repetition and layout on the page to create your poetic effects.)

Write a spell for one of the things you discussed by building on this suggestion:

Gruesome Ingredients

To (*write here what you want the spell to do*)
Take five squashed bluebottles
One cowpat
Three toadstools
   etc.

Mix them up and drink them down
And your wish will be granted within the hour
(If you are still alive!)

Albanac's spell calls on the power of wind, wrath, fire, etc. Jot down other things which have power and use them to add extra lines to the spell. Perhaps the extra lines will make the spell work. If so, you will need to write a different ending and invent three different magic words.

Using the words you jotted down, and anything you wish to borrow from Albanac's spell, complete this spell:

May the power of —————————,
The power of —————————,
   etc.
And the power of —————————
(*Write here what you want the spell to do*).

Some of the spells make use of strange-sounding magic words. Find out which these are and re-read them, then try making up some magic words of your own and write spells to go with them. If you can't think of any, try using a dictionary. Jozef found the magic words for his 'Birthday Spell' at the back of his dictionary in one of the special supplements of unusual words.

Poetry Puzzle

Can you help the witch in this picture? She wants to cast a spell, but can't find her spell book, and doesn't know which ingredients to use! Write the spell for her (you'll have to guess what she wants it to do!). You can use for ingredients anything that you can see in the picture (even her stool if necessary!) but nothing else (she's not going to the witches' supermarket this week!).

4
Spooky Snapshots

Out of film? Try a
Seventeen-syllable verse
Snapshot—a haiku!

Cars and videos are not the only things imported from Japan. The haiku is a Japanese poetic form which was imported earlier this century because of its exceptional compactness. It is a complete poem of just seventeen syllables, divided into three lines of five, seven and five syllables. A haiku is like a snapshot—it captures a scene in a small space. Only the essentials are given; the rest is left to the reader's imagination, as in this example:

Footsteps on the stairs	(5)
A murmur, a sigh, a knock—	(7)
But no one is there!	(5)

Writing an exact number of syllables is a good preparation for more difficult kinds of poetry, and the discipline of fitting your ideas into so small a space will teach you not to waste words—a lesson that will improve your English generally!

But be warned! These Japanese mini-poems can be catching, and you may find, like the second year pupils who wrote the ones below, that once you start writing them you won't be able to stop!

Ghosts, ghouls, all whirring,
Scaring us out of our house,
Slamming doors deftly.

Steve Crane

The graveyard—silent,
A shadow in the dimness
Which creeps up behind.

Nina Stafford

Fear
Shivers down the spine,
Butterflies in the stomach,
Cold sweat on the brow.

Steven Scogings

Storm clouds gathering
The forest sighs in the wind
A screech from a crow.

David Piatto

There was half a moon
Shining bright in the night,
And wolves howling.

Sheryl Robinson

The dental surgeon
With his mouth-murdering tools—
Oh no!—It's my turn!

Caroline Hilton

TIPS FOR WRITING

One of the haikus above does not obey the syllable rule. Which one is it and how much does it vary from the pattern?

It is probable that you had to count the syllables of every haiku before you could answer the last question. This shows that it is not essential to obey the syllable rule. Many good haikus have been written which don't. So, while it is a useful discipline to try to write the set number of syllables in each line, don't throw away a good haiku because of a few syllables more or less.

Note how the title of the haiku by Steven Scogings adds to the meaning of the poem. With such a small space in which to express yourself, a carefully chosen title can be a great help.

If you can't find a word with the right number of syllables, use a thesaurus to look up words of similar meaning with different numbers of syllables.

Try extending some of your haikus into longer poems.

Compile a class album of spooky snapshots.

Poetry Puzzle

Try to add that extra touch of authenticity to your haikus by rewriting them using Japanese characters. This is not as easy as it sounds. Japanese characters are quite different from the letters of our alphabet because they often stand for whole syllables, as you can see from the table below. The difference is so great that you will have to adapt and even invent characters to supply the missing sounds.

Jap Char	Sound	Jap Char	Sound	Jap Char	Sound
ア	a	チ	chi	ム	mu
イ	i	ツ	tsu	メ	me
ウ	u	テ	te	モ	mo
エ	e	ト	to	ヤ	ya
オ	o	ナ	na	ユ	yu
カ	ka	ニ	ni	ヨ	yo
キ	ki	ヌ	nu	ラ	ra
ク	ku	ネ	ne	リ	ri
ケ	ke	ノ	no	ル	ru
コ	ko	ハ	fa(ha)	レ	re
サ	sa	ヒ	fi(hi)	ロ	ro
シ	shi	フ	fu	ワ	wa
ス	su	ヘ	fe(he)	ヱ	we
セ	se	ホ	fo(ho)	ヰ	wi
ソ	so	マ	ma	ヲ	wo
タ	ta	ミ	mi	—	—

5
Clerihews

Those of you who have been itching to use rhyme will be pleased to know that, as from now, the ban on rhyme is lifted! We are going to study its use in the simplest form possible—the clerihew. These funny four-line poems are named after their inventor, Edmund *Clerihew* Bentley, and are usually about a famous person, whose name ends the first line. The second line has to rhyme with the first (two lines which rhyme in this way are called a couplet). Much of the humour of the clerihew arises from the need to find a rhyme for a person's name, which can be quite difficult (that's why there aren't many clerihews about William the Conqueror!).

> Sir Christopher Wren
> Said, 'I am going to dine with some men.
> If anybody calls
> Say I am designing St Paul's.'
>
> Edmund Clerihew Bentley

The four lines can be of any length (though they are usually fairly short) so there is no need to worry about rhythm or the number of syllables. This allows you to concentrate fully on rhyme, and you will need to concentrate to use rhyme effectively! Rhyme is difficult for an English poet because our language has many words for which there are very few rhymes—or none at all! For this reason it is particularly important to observe these two rules:

Rhymes must sound perfectly natural—*never* use an unsuitable word just because it rhymes.
Rhymes shouldn't lead you to say something you didn't intend to say.

Fortunately, the clerihew is an exception to the second rule. You will notice from the following examples that you can allow the rhyme to lead the meaning. The whole point of the clerihew is to develop the humorous ideas suggested by the rhymes—you don't have to be factually or historically accurate!

Edward the Confessor
Slept under the dresser.
When that began to pall,
He slept in the hall.

Edmund Clerihew Bentley

Mr Bram Stoker
Was a bit of a joker;
Either that or he
Had bats in his belfrey.

Charles Connell

The Art of Biography
Is different from Geography.
Geography is about Maps,
Biography is about Chaps.

Edmund Clerihew Bentley

Schubert is shown in his prime
In 'Lilac Time'.
His ardour's diminished
In 'The Unfinished'.

Coleridge, Samuel Taylor,
Wrote about an old sailor.
As a Coleridge fan,
I prefer 'Kubla Khan'.

Charles Connell

Here are some clerihews written by pupils in a third year English lesson:

King Canute
Got a new suit
But it was spoiled because he
Tried to turn back the sea.

Mark Kerridge

Sir Francis Drake
Learned to sail on a lake—
But defeating the Armada
Was much harder!

Nicholas Appleby

Queen Elizabeth the First
Had a great thirst
So she rushed to the pub
And ordered a pint and some grub.

Mandy Fowler

Humphrey Bogart
Auditioned for a part
In 'Casablanca'—
He had to say, 'Here's lookin' at ya'.'

Mandy Fowler

Bugs Bunny
Thought it was funny
To play in the snow,
But his paws didn't think so!

Matthew Gort

History
Is a mystery.
Everyone thinks it's boring
And ends up snoring.

Nicholas Key

WRITING

How many rhymes can you find for these words?

day   love   juice   nation   picture   cycle   typist

Jot down several names—pop stars, politicians, cartoon characters, historical figures, etc. Look over them and see which one suggests a rhyme with amusing possibilities. Develop the idea in lines three and four.

If you can't find a rhyme, try turning the name round, as in the clerihew about Coleridge above, or try ending the line with another word, as in the clerihew about Schubert.

The clerihew about Biography and Geography shows that you don't have to have a name as a subject. Used in this way a clerihew is just a short, humorous poem. Try writing clerihews on a range of different subjects.

A Rhyme Puzzle

> What is the rhyme for porringer?
> What is the rhyme for porringer?
> The King he had a daughter fair
> And gave the Prince of Orange her.

Traditional

Note that the third line does not rhyme, and the fourth line rhymes with the first two. It must rhyme *exactly*. If it is a two syllable word, both syllables must rhyme. For example, beauty/duty. Rhymes of two and three syllables are the most effective.

Try to complete this:

> What is the rhyme for History?
> What is the rhyme for History?
>
> _____
>
> _____

Try others based on these words:

> spooky   money   donkey   itchiness   kissable   royalty

Make up a first line for your friend to complete. There is only one rule—you must be able to complete it yourself (i.e. there must be at least one rhyme—however far-fetched).

6
Limericks

A skeleton once in Khartoum
Invited a ghost to his room.
   They spent the whole night
   In the eeriest fight
As to who should be frightened of whom.

                  Anon

The limerick is an even funnier verse form than the clerihew. This is because it has a humorous, bouncy rhythm to go with its humorous rhymes. Writing limericks is a good way to begin learning about rhythm in poetry. A detailed study of rhythm would be very complicated, involving things such as trochees and dactyls (which sound a bit like prehistoric monsters, and can be just as daunting!). Fortunately, it is quite easy to get the rhythm right by 'ear'. If you read through the limericks in this chapter, especially if you read them aloud, you will soon get used to the rhythm or 'beat' of limericks and be able to write them easily.

As well as listening for the rhythm, note how rhyme has been used. Some writers set themselves the problem of finding rhymes for a difficult word, such as 'Uttoxeter' and then amaze and amuse us by their ability to find suitable rhymes—and tell a joke at the same time!

There was a young girl of Uttoxeter,
Who worked nine to five as a choc-setter;
   She rolled the chocks thin
   With a wee rolling-pin,
So they'd fit in the After Eight box better.

                  Anon

There was a young lady of Ryde,
Who ate some green apples and died.
   The apples fermented
   Inside the lamented,
And made cider inside her inside.

                  Anon

There was a young man of Calcutta,
Who had a most terrible stutta,
   He said: 'Pass the h. . .ham,
   And the j. . .j. . .j. . .jam,
And the b. . .b. . .b. . .b. . .butta'.

Anon

There was an old man of Dunoon
Who always ate soup with a fork.
   For he said: 'As I eat
   Neither fish, fowl, nor flesh,
I should otherwise finish too quick'.

Anon

LIMERICKS BY EDWARD LEAR

There was an old man of Cape Horn,
Who wished he had never been born:
   So he sat on a chair,
   Till he died of despair,
That dolorous old man of Cape Horn.

There was an old man in a tree,
Who was horribly stung by a bee;
   When they said: 'Does it buzz?'
   He replied: 'Yes, it does,
It's a regular brute of a bee!'

LIMERICKS BY PUPILS

There was a young fellow from Leeds
Who ate a whole packet of seeds,
   In less than an hour
   His nose was a flower
And his head was a garden of weeds.

Stephanie Gander, aged 12

There was an old man of Peru
Who was sick with a touch of the flu,
   He puked on the stairs
   And all over the chairs
Before he could get to the loo.

Nicholas Appleby, aged 13

There was an old lady from Leigh
Who ate pickled eggs for her tea
   She ate them with mustard
   And sometimes with custard
And sometimes with pussycat's pee.

Eloise Judd, aged 12

There was an old fellow of York
Who took up his knife and his fork
   And tucked into his lamb
   Which was covered with jam
And was followed by custard on pork.

Mark Kerridge, aged 13

There was a young man from New Hampton
Who made his way home with a lantern.
    The lantern went out
    And the man gave a shout—
'I hope I don't meet with a phantom!'

Claire Gunn, aged 13

STUDYING THE RHYTHM

It is quite easy to get the rhythm of a limerick right by 'ear'. However, it is useful to study the rhythm in detail, as this will help you to put right the occasional problem line, and will lay a valuable foundation for later study.

First of all, copy out the limerick that begins the chapter. Then read it aloud, listening for the 'beat'. The beat has the effect of emphasising certain syllables. Try to hear which syllables these are, and mark them with a diagonal stroke like this:

A skeleton once in Khartoum

Count up the number of beats in each line and you will see the pattern.

IDEAS FOR WRITING

'There was an old man of Dunoon' doesn't rhyme at all, and yet its humour depends on rhyme. Read it through in pairs and try to be aware of what your brain *wants* to read because of the influence of the well-known rhyme scheme, then discuss how the humour works.

Now re-write the limerick so that it rhymes. Does it still make sense?

Complete these limericks:

I sat next to a Duchess at tea,
Distressed as a person could be.
    Her rumblings abdominal
    Were simply phenomenal—
_____

I'm a pupil at ——————— School
And the head teacher thinks I'm a fool

—————————————————————

—————————————————————

—————————————————————

Now you're on your own, but here's two final tips to help you. If you find, as many limerick writers do, that the last line is the most difficult part to get right, look at Edward Lear's limericks and see how he solved that problem.

Another useful trick is to end the first line with a place name (as in many of the above examples) but to leave the writing of the first line until last. Then you can invent one to fit the other two rhymes (or find a suitable place name from an atlas—in the whole world there must be a place name to rhyme with *anything*!).

FOLLOW-UP WORK

Make a collection of limericks from various sources including some written by yourself and your friends.

Poetry Puzzle

The lines of these limericks have been jumbled up together. Sort them out into their proper order:

There was an old lady from China
As big as a house
Who flew to the moon in a plane
She slipped on the deck
And now she's as light as a feather

There was a young woman called Jane
Who had come to the end of her tether
She went on a diet
And twisted her neck
And ended up going insane

There was a fat lady called Heather
She saw a moon-mouse
Who sailed in a big ocean liner
(Though she's keeping it quiet)
and now all she sees is behind her

Jumble up some of the limericks in this book for your friends to unravel.
Try to make them tell a story (however nonsensical!).

7
Mother Shipton— Prophetess or Witch?

Ursula Sonthiel, later known as Mother Shipton, was born in 1488. She soon gained a reputation for being able to foretell the future, and people came from miles around to consult her. Some of the prophecies attributed to her are said to have come true. Read the ones given below and form your own opinion.

Carriages without horses will go,
And accidents fill the world with woe.
Primrose Hill in London shall be
And in its centre a Bishop's See.
Around the world thoughts shall fly
In the twinkling of an eye.
Water shall yet more wonders do,
How strange, yet shall be true.
The world upside down shall be,
And gold found at the root of a tree.
Through hills men shall ride
And no horse or ass be by their side,
Under water men shall walk
Shall ride, shall sleep, and talk;
In the air men shall be seen,
In white, in black, and in green.
A great man shall come and go—
Three times shall lovely France
Be led to play a bloody dance
Before her people shall be free.
Three tyrant Rulers shall she see,
Three times the people's hope is gone,

Three Rulers in succession see,
Each springing from different dynasty.
Then shall the worser fight be done,
England and France shall be as one.
The British Olive next shall twine
In marriage with the German vine.
Men shall walk over rivers and under rivers,
Iron in the water shall float,
As easy as a wooden boat;
Gold shall be found, and found
In a land that's not now known.
Fire and water shall more wonders do
England shall at last admit a Jew:
The Jew that was held in scorn
Shall of a Christian be born and born.
A house of glass shall come to pass
In England, but alas!
War will follow with the work,
In the land of Pagan and Turk,
And State and State in fierce strife,
Will seek each other's life.
But when the North shall divide the South
An eagle shall build in the lion's mouth.
Taxes for blood and for war,
Will come to every door.
All England's sons that plough the land,
Shall be seen, book in hand:
Learning shall so ebb and flow,
The poor shall most learning know.
Waters shall flow where corn shall grow,
Corn shall grow where waters doth flow,
Houses shall appear in the vales below,
And covered by hail and snow;
The world then to an end shall come.

STUDYING THE RHYTHM AND RHYME

The basic rhythmic pattern of this poem is a line of eight syllables with four stresses. The stresses are marked with a diagonal line.

> The British Olive next shall twine   (8 syllables)
>
> In marriage with the German vine.   (8 syllables)

But Mother Shipton has allowed herself a great deal of flexibility: the number of syllables in a line varies from six to twelve, though the number of stresses is usually four per line, enabling the poem to flow smoothly.

You can check this for yourself by copying out a number of lines, counting the syllables and marking in the stresses. Remember that the best way to hear the stresses is to read the poem aloud.

Now check the rhyme scheme. Note any variations from the pattern of couplets, and any rhymes which are not exact.

You will notice once again that there is a great deal of flexibility. Mother Shipton has varied the rigid pattern of the rhyming eight-syllable couplet in order to express her ideas more freely. This flexibility is called 'poetic licence' and you should make full use of it yourself.

DISCUSSION

Which of these prophecies seem to have come true?

Are there any prophecies which seem vague, or little more than intelligent guesses?

Judging from the evidence before you, do you think that Mother Shipton really had the ability to see into the future?

What does Mother Shipton prophesy will happen just before the end of the world?

Have any of these events happened already?

What do you think will happen in the future?

WRITING

Using rhyming couplets, write your own prophecies for the future. Try to get a sense of rhythm into your lines, and remember to use poetic licence where necessary. Write a short poem to begin with, but you will soon find that couplets will flow easily and that you can write longer poems.

Find other poems written in couplets (there are several in this book) and note how couplets can be grouped in many different ways. A single couplet is often used for an epigram or epitaph. Two, four or six couplets can be grouped together to make verses of different lengths, and, of course, any number of couplets can be grouped together to make one long poem. Write a number of poems using couplets in as many different ways as possible.

Poetry Puzzle

Add your ingredients to this spell to destroy school by filling in the gaps:

Throw into the magic pot
Teachers, prefects—all the lot!

Throw your ——————— in the brew

Throw in all your ——————— too!

Add a dash of ———————

And ———————
Throw into the magic pot
Teachers, prefects—all the lot!

Stir into the steaming slime

———————————————

Don't forget to add ———————

And ———————
Throw into the magic pot
Teachers, prefects—all the lot!

While you stir, recite this spell:

———————————————

———————————————

———————————————

Throw into the magic pot
Teachers, prefects—all the lot!

Finish off with a verse or two of your own. Do it well enough and it might even work—if you can get the ingredients that is!

8
Ballads

The people of long ago had the same appetite for horror stories as people today, but of course, they couldn't see them on television as you might do—they couldn't even read them, because most people in those days never learned to read or write. They relied on ballads—traditional verse stories passed on by word of mouth, which would be sung or recited during an evening's entertainment. Occasionally they may have been lucky enough to hear a ballad recited by one of the professional minstrels who wandered over Europe in the Middle Ages earning a living by telling tales of heroes, battles, romance and the supernatural.

Most of these romantic figures have been forgotten, but a few names have come down to us because of their connection with kings and great events of the past. One such was Ivo Taillefer, minstrel to William the Conqueror, who recited 'Le Chanson de Roland' at the Battle of Hastings to inspire William's knights. Another was Blondel, minstrel to King Richard the Lionheart, who when his master was imprisoned sought him everywhere in Europe, singing songs of the Aquitaine countryside, until one day he got a reply from his master from behind a barred window.

Professional ballad singers may still be found in many countries today, especially in places where modern mass media has made little impression and the oral tradition is still strong.

Ballads were composed in many different forms. One verse form, in which the second and fourth lines rhyme, is so common that it has become known as 'ballad form'. This form is used in 'The Ballad of the Demon Lover'. Another common form is a four-line verse made up of two couplets. Alison Rostron used this form to write 'The Great Whale'. Many other variations are possible.

The Ballad of the Demon Lover

'O where have you been, my long, long love,
    This long seven years and more?'
'O I'm come to seek my former vows,
    Ye granted me before.'

'O hold your tongue of your former vows,
    For they will breed sad strife,
O hold your tongue of your former vows,
    For I am become a wife.'

He turned him right and round about,
    And the tear blinded his eye.
'I would never have trodden on Irish ground,
    If it had not been for thee.'

'If I was to leave my husband dear,
    And my two babes also,
O what have you to take me to,
    If with you I should go?'

'I have seven ships upon the sea,
    The eighth brought me to land,
With four-and-twenty bold mariners,
    And music on every hand.'

She has taken up her two little babes,
    Kissed them both cheek and chin,
'O fare ye well, my own two babes,
    For I'll never see you again.'

She set her foot upon the ship,
    No mariners could she behold,
But the sails were made of taffeta
    And the masts of beaten gold.

They had not sailed a league, a league,
    A league but barely three,
When she espied his cloven foot,
    And she wept right bitterly.

'O hold your tongue of your weeping,' says he,
  'Of your weeping now let me be,
I will show you how the lilies grow
  On the banks of Italy.'

'O what hills are yon, yon pleasant hills,
  That the sun shines sweetly on?'
'O yon are the hills of heaven,' he said,
  'Which you will never win.'

'O what a mountain is yon,' she said,
  'All so dreary with frost and snow?'
'O yon is the mountain of hell,' he cried,
  'Where you and I will go.'

And whenever she turned her round about,
  The taller he seemed to be,
Until that the tops of the gallant ship
  No taller were than he.

He struck the topmast with his hand,
  The foremast with his knee,
And he brake that gallant ship in twain,
  And sank her in the sea.

Anon

The Great Whale

White canvas clouds go sailing by,
Serenely under the clouds of the sky,
A whaling ship, carrying barrels so full
With the oil of a sperm whale that's valuable still.

'Tis a strong wind that drives the ship forward in might,
'Tis a bright sun that shines down and produces the light
For to see a white palm tree of runaway steam
Of a sea-giant breaking—'A great whale been seen!'

On the brown sun-baked decks there stand unruly whalers
Awaiting the order to allow every sailor
To spring into action: to board every boat
And to stab every harpoon in a bull sperm whale's throat.

From the small quarter-deck comes a deep-throated order!
You, you, you, and you, to the 'Seagull' and board her!
The quartet by the rail, why you go and follow
And the next eight I choose can go boarding the Swallow.

The men so dispatched, they run off to their boats
Resounding splashes as they launch and float,
Oars are snatched up and dug into the sea
As the small boats reluctantly—with anxiety

Slide forward to meet the great bulk of the whale,
Who feels somewhat suspicious and twitches his tail.
The small boats creep nearer, who is to go first?
Each harpoonist is eager, but under a curse.

As the whale rears and dives down—where to? Who could
say?
But Leviathan himself, the black shadow of day,
Only he knows what will happen when he
Breaks up all emotions and comes up from the sea.

Harpoons go swinging in, embedded in the mountain
Red stains the steam of the ever-on fountain.
The great whale turns head on the offending boats
And rolls over on them, no more will they float.

Splintered wood floats over the sea,
The mother ship welcomes her cubs of the sea,
And so many deaths have been caused by the sea,
And a long hunted beast who inherits the sea.

Alison Rostron, aged 11

The Curse of Rose Hall

Darkness hangs thick on the haunted air
And a ghostly jury in session there
Lays Annie Palmer's foul deeds bare
   In the ruined rooms of Rose Hall.

Oh white in the daylight the stone walls gleam
And gracious and spacious the vast rooms seem
And the poisons and murderings all a dream,
   And the frightened ghosts of Rose Hall.

But on moonless evenings when Patoo calls
And no clear brightness from heaven falls
Then into the ruins of splendid halls
   Slink the vengeful ghosts of Rose Hall.

Up from its cellars and nameless graves
Slouch husband, and lovers, and strong black slaves.
And she looks in vain for the face that saves.
   But each wants revenge for Rose Hall.

The deadly evidence tolls its bell
As one by one the victims tell
Of how they lived in that witch's hell
   With the wicked Queen of Rose Hall.

Proud Annie hears what they tell about
And she savagely tries to curse them out,
But nobody there can hear her shout.
   For all are dead at Rose Hall.

With fury she listens to their tale
And not for repentance does she pale—
But to know that her obeah could fail,
   And bring her death at Rose Hall.

When the last of the shuddering victims spoke
The jury its ghostly silence broke,
And bound the White Witch with a fearful yoke
   To the ruined stones of Rose Hall.

Now on secret nights when the sky is blind
And Patoo mocks what his sharp eyes find
You can hear Annie's bitter sobs behind
    The crumbling walls of Rose Hall.

                  Alma Norman

Arthur and the Vampire

Arthur looked up
As the vampire swooped
And Arthur fled
From the gruesome undead!

Out of breath Arthur
Tried to run faster
But oh my God!
What a disaster!

The poor man tripped,
Stumbled and fell,
The vampire stood over him
Eyes raging like hell.

Arthur knew his fate was near
So he knelt on his knees
And started to pray
For the arrival of day.

Arthur crouched low
And pulled out a knife,
The vampire removed his mask
And said—'Arthur, this is your life!'

    Neil Cornwell, Karl Cross
    and Peter Berry, aged 13

STUDYING THE RHYTHM AND RHYME

Copy out the first three verses of 'The Ballad of the Demon Lover', count the syllables in each line and mark the stressed syllables as you did in Chapter Seven.

Look at the rhyme scheme of each ballad. Which lines rhyme? Which rhymes are not quite exact, showing that the poet made use of the extra flexibility allowed by poetic licence?

IDEAS FOR WRITING

The ballad verse form in which the second and fourth lines rhyme is one of the commonest in English poetry, and has been used for poems of just one verse to ballads several pages long. Find other examples of its use (there are several in this book) and experiment with short poems before trying a full length ballad. If you wish you can use a four-line verse made up of two couplets as Alison Rostron has done in 'The Great Whale'. You can even mix the two verse forms as in 'Arthur and the Vampire'. The important thing is the vigour and excitement of the story.

GROUP WORK

Writing a full length story in verse can be a daunting prospect, and it is therefore a good idea to share the work among a group of four or five pupils. After an initial planning session, different members of your group could write different parts of the ballad, the final stage being to edit the whole ballad together.

Poetry Puzzle

The title has been removed from this poem, making it into a kind of riddle. What is the creature in the poem, and what was the title?

When fishes flew and forests walked
And figs grew upon thorn,
Some moment when the moon was blood
Then surely I was born:

With monstrous head and sickening cry
And ears like errant wings,
The devil's walking parody
On all four-footed things.

The tattered outlaw of the earth,
Of ancient crooked will;
Starve, scourge, deride me; I am dumb.
I keep my secret still.

Fools! For I also had my hour;
One far fierce hour and sweet:
There was a shout about my ears,
And palms before my feet.

G.K. Chesterton

Find other poems which can be made into riddles by removing the title, and try them on your friends.

9
Acrostic Poems

Try to work out for yourself what an acrostic poem is from this example by Lewis Carroll. It was sent to a girl with the present of a book entitled *The Hunt of the Snark*. The girl's name is hidden somewhere in the poem. See if you can find it.

Acrostic

'Are you deaf, Father William!' the young man said,
'Did you hear what I told you just now?
'Excuse me for shouting! Don't waggle your head
'Like a blundering, sleepy old cow!
'A little maid dwelling in Wallington Town,
'Is my friend, so I beg to remark:
'Do you think she'd be pleased if a book were sent down
'Entitled "The Hunt of the Snark?" '

'Pack it up in brown paper!' the old man cried,
'And seal it with olive-and-dove.
'I command you to do it!' he added with pride,
'Nor forget, my good fellow, to send her beside
'Easter Greetings, and give her my love.'

Did you manage to work it out? If so, you are now ready to write some acrostic poems of your own—but don't worry!—you are not expected to write something as difficult as this with the added problems of rhythm and rhyme! You should aim at something simpler to begin with, based on a short word. Use free verse, keep the lines fairly short, and resist the temptation to use rhyme—you'll find enough problems fitting the acrostic!

Here are some examples written by pupils:

Vicious beings in the night,
A bat swoops past your head,
Maybe it's not what it seems,
Perhaps it's your uncle George instead.
I always thought him rather funny,
Reading books whilst standing upside down—
Easy for a vampire!

Claire Gunn, aged 13

Never had I seen such horrors,
I ran as fast as I could go,
Glancing back to see the mutated man,
Horror once more filled my heart,
Trembling I staggered to a forbidding door,
My fingers grasped the handle,
A feeling of relief as the door swings open
Re-awakening me, still trembling,
Even though I know it was just a dream.

Zak Fettroll, aged 15

Pale and very faint
He glides through the corridors
And there is
No hope for him, suffering endless
Torment.
On and on he goes through the rooms,
Maybe one day he will find peace of mind.

Mark Kerridge, aged 13

Gloomy is this place:
Ravens are circling and slowly
Approaching—or are they
Vampires, bloodthirsty and
Evil—I don't wait to find out!

Stephen Sullivan, aged 12

Gruesome tales,
Haunted houses,
Objects moving,
Spirits speaking,
Tombs creaking,
Skeletons muttering.

Victoria Brown, aged 13

IDEAS FOR WRITING

Jot down words which would make suitable acrostics. Here are some suggestions:

bat   evil   bones   witch   ghost   terror   vampire

When you are fairly good at writing short acrostics, try some longer ones:

mouldering graves (two verses)
heaven and hell (three verses)

Write some acrostics based on names. Using your own name, write an acrostic for a Valentine card (and send it, next February 14th!). Use your friend's name for a birthday card acrostic. Christmas cards and Mother's Day cards provide other opportunities. (You couldn't do much worse than the rubbishy verse that usually appears on such cards!)

Acrostics can be effectively combined with riddles, the acrostic providing a hidden answer. If you want to disguise the acrostic, try indenting the lines, like this:

Brilliant mini-sun
    under man's control,
lacking the candle's loveliness—
    but a lot brighter!

Creeping along the fence
    alert for sound and movement
trying to pick up a mouse's scent.

Chris Bonard, aged 14

Poetry Puzzle

This poem by Lewis Carroll is a mixture of a riddle and an acrostic. The answer is two girls' names. When you have puzzled out how it works, try to write one of your own and give it to a friend to solve.

Double Acrostic

Two little girls near London dwell,
More naughty than I like to tell.
        [1]
Upon the lawn the hoops are seen:
The balls are rolling on the green.   T ur F
        [2]
The Thames is running deep and wide:
And boats are rowing on the tide.   R ive R
        [3]
In winter-time, all in a row,
The happy skaters come and go.   I c E
        [4]
'Papa!' they cry, 'Do let us stay!'
He does not speak, but says they may.   N o D
        [5]
'There is a land,' he says, 'my dear,
Which is too hot to skate, I fear.'   A fric A

10
Alphabets

A Horror Alphabet

All the horrors from A–Z
Tormented me last night in bed:

Apparitions
Bats and bloodthirsty banshees
Creepy-crawly coffin worms
Demons and devils
Evil Esperanto-speaking elves
F
G
H
I
J
K
L
M
N

O
P
Q
R
S
T
U
V
W
X
Y
Z

All the horrors from A–Z
Tormented me last night in bed.

(I'm not sleeping in that room again!)

Complete this horror alphabet. Where appropriate, add descriptive words beginning with the same letter, for example, 'bloodthirsty banshees', 'creepy-crawly coffin-worms'. This creates an effect called 'alliteration' which we shall be looking at in more detail in the next chapter. You should be able to find at least one horror for every letter of the alphabet, as well as descriptive words to go with them. For the more difficult letters, or if you get stuck for an idea, use a dictionary.

Read these examples of different kinds of alphabet poem, and then try some of your own.

Animal Alphabet

You go to a zoo
To look at the animals,
But they're all looking at you!

Antelopes stare at you,
Baboons and bullocks glare at you,
Cats and cobras look at you as if to say 'silly moo!'
Dogs and dingos howl at you,
Elephants spray water at you,
Fish blow bubbles at you,
Gorillas growl and roar at you,
Hippopotamuses yawn at you,
Insects hum and buzz at you,
Jaguars snarl and hiss at you,
Koala bears smile at you,
Lions are so proud they just ignore you,
Monkeys laugh and make faces at you,
Newts splash and wriggle at you,
Octopi wave their arms at you,
Parrots hurl abuse at you,
Quails flutter and flap at you,
Rattlesnakes bare their fangs at you,
Seals call and clap at you,
Tarantulas creep menacingly towards you,
Unicorns puzzle you (because you thought they didn't exist!)
Venomous snakes spit at you,
Whales spout at you,
X . . . . (This creature's name is a secret!)
Yaks moo at you,
Zoo-keepers keep their eye on you.

You go to a zoo
To look at the animals,
But they're all looking at you!

Zoe Goodall, aged 12

56

Neil Cornwell, aged 14

The ABC

'Twas midnight in the schoolroom
And every desk was shut,
When suddenly from the alphabet
Was heard a loud 'Tut-tut!'

Said A to B, 'I don't like C;
His manners are a lack.
For all I ever see of C
Is a semicircular back!'

'I disagree,' said D to B,
'I've never found C so.
From where *I* stand, he seems to be
An uncompleted O.'

C was vexed. 'I'm much perplexed,
You criticise my shape.
I'm made like that, to help spell Cat
And Cow and Cool and Cape.'

'He's right,' said E; said F, 'Whoopee!'
Said G, ' 'Ip, 'ip, 'ooray!'
'You're dropping me,' roared H to G.
'Don't do it please, I pray!'

'Out of my way,' LL said to K.
'I'll make poor I look Ill.'
To stop this stunt, J stood in front,
And presto! ILL was JILL.

'U know,' said V, 'that W
Is twice the age of me,
For as a Roman V is five
I'm half as young as he.'

X and Y yawned sleepily,
'Look at the time!' they said.
They all jumped in to beddy byes
And the last one in was Z!

Spike Milligan

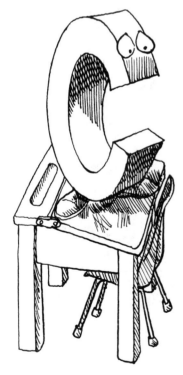

Miss Ellen Gee of Kew

Peerless yet hopeless maid of Q,
  Accomplish'd L N G,
Never again shall I and U
  Together sip our T.
For oh! the fates, I know not Y,
  Sent 'midst the flowers a B;
Which ven'mous stung her in the I,
  So that she could not C.
    L N exclaimed, 'Vile spiteful B,
      If ever I catch U
    On jessmine, rosebud or sweet P,
      I'll change your singing Q.'

                Anon

Poetry Puzzle

We take for granted the twenty-six letters which we use to write down our ideas, but there are many other types of writing, and it can be great fun to experiment with them. A particularly interesting example is Easter Island script, which was used long ago by the Polynesian people of Easter Island. It has not yet been deciphered.

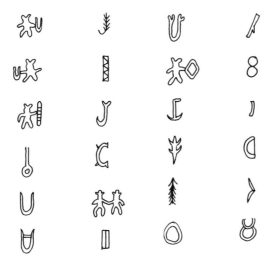

Many of these signs are simplified pictures. What pictures can you make out, and what do you think each sign may mean?

Copy out the script, give letter values to each sign (this, of course, will be pure guesswork!) and write messages and poems in them.

Find out about other types of writing (see page 28). You could also try making up your own alphabets—use these to rewrite some of your spells (see Chapter Three).

11
Alliteration

When you were writing your alphabet poems, you may have noticed a pleasing musical effect when words beginning with the same sound were used together:

Weird witches and wizened wizards working spells with worms, winkles and whippets.

Other examples can be found in a surprising number of places:

In adverts

KARATE KIDS!

Look In, 31st May 1986

Best, better, British?

What Hi Fi?, March 1985

In newspapers

MOTEL MADNESS...

SOMETHING strange is happening at Crossroads. Jill has taken to dressing like a prison warder. Nicola sounds like Margaret Thatcher – and Kath Brownlow is getting engaged. Even Benny is not quite himself. He has started shaving every day.

The Star, 17th September 1986

In magazines

BUDGET BEATERS

Beat the budget blues and stay on top! We've rounded up the latest, brightest looks in town at prices you can afford

Woman's Own, 8th March 1986

Meet Brother Crispin, who makes sure KP are the crispiest crisps ever created.

in newspaper headlines: 'Motel Murder Mystery'
in advertisements: 'Meet Brother Crispin, who makes sure KP are the crispiest
    crisps ever created.'
in well-known sayings: 'Time and tide wait for no man.'
in tongue-twisters: 'The sixth sick sheik's sixth sheep's sick.'
and, of course, in poetry.

This effect is called *alliteration*. Like rhyme, it is a musical effect which can be used to add beauty or emphasis. In fact the earliest English poets, such as the unknown Beowulf poet, preferred alliteration to rhyme and their poems provide perhaps the best example of its use. If it is overdone it can make a poem amusingly difficult to read aloud. This, of course, is the basis of many tongue-twisters (see page 65) but would spoil the effect of a serious poem.

Wild Witches' Ball

late last night at wildwitchhall
we witches held our wild witch ball.
in every size and shape and weight
we witches came to celebrate.

ten tall crones with moans and groans
battled in barrels with bats and bones.
nine queer dears with pointed ears
dangled and swang from the chandeliers.

witches eight with mangy tresses
danced with seven sorceresses.
witches six in shaggy rags
played toss and tag with five old hags.

four fat bags took healthy bites
from parts of three unsightly frights.
two fierce furies dug a ditch
and tumbled in one lumpy witch.

there were witches squeezed in every nook
whichever where you cared to look.
how many witches can you see
at our annual wildwitch witches' spree?

Jack Prelutsky

Beowulf's Fight with the Dragon

The treasure-guardian heard the talk
Of Beowulf, and breathed his burning breath.
The warrior fought to fend off the fire,
Brandished the bright blade of his sword,
And held his shield against the shower of sparks.
Then Fate gave him his chance for fame,
A chance to deal a death-blow to the dragon:
He struck the scaly serpent with his sword—
But the bright edge did not bite into the bone
And the Geat's lord lay in peril of his life.
The treasure-guardian triumphed to see his trouble
And flung far-leaping war-flames at his foe.
Badly burned, Beowulf was forced from the battle—
His sword had failed him in his hour of need.

Anglo-Saxon

Hinx, Minx, the Old Witch Winks

Hinx, minx, the old witch winks,
The fat begins to fry.
Nobody at home but jumping Joan,
Father, mother and I.
Stick, stock, stone dead,
Blind man can't see:
Every knave will have a slave,
You and I must be he.

Anon

Reasons for Extinction

Dodos do
nothing to
dastards who
do dodos down.

Dog-god does
not defend
dodos being
undone.

Dodos lovey-dovey
with dodo darlings
don't become
dodo dams or dads.

Dodos do
dumb things
like Dido or
dinosaurs did.

So dodos die
out.

H.O. Nazareth

Moths and Moonshine

Moths and moonshine mean to me
Magic—madness—mystery.

Witches dancing weird and wild
Mischief make for man and child.

Owls screech from woodland shades,
Moths glide through moonlit glades,

Moving in dark and secret wise
Like a plotter in disguise.

Moths and moonshine mean to me
Magic—madness—mystery.

James Reeves

Willy the Wally

Willy is a wally
He walks with a waddle
Like a wallaby in wellingtons.

Willy is a wally
He wears weird woollies
That make him look like a werewolf.

Willy is a wally
He tries to be wise and witty
But ends up even more widiculous!

Simon Weston, aged 13

THINGS TO DO

Copy out 'Moths and Moonshine' and underline the letters which alliterate. Now read the poem aloud, listening to the effect of the alliteration.

Find examples of alliteration in newspaper headlines and advertisements. Cut them out and make a wall display. Think of more examples of well-known sayings which use alliteration. Write them out and add them to the display.

Make up some alliterative newspaper headlines and advertising slogans. Add them to your wall display.

Write some short poems of your own. To begin with, write poems without rhyme so that you can concentrate on the alliteration. Then you can try combining alliteration with rhyme.

Write some more alphabet poems (or revise the ones you've written) concentrating on alliteration.

If you can't think of a word to alliterate with another, try browsing through the appropriate section of a dictionary. Not only will you find the word you want, it may also suggest other ideas—and widen your vocabulary into the bargain!

TONGUE-TWISTERS

Swan swam over the sea,
Swim, swan, swim.
Swan swam back again,
Well swum swan.

Anon

Silly Shelly shovels sand on the sea-shore.

Hayley Bradley, aged 11

Nasty Nora nicked nice Nicola's knickers.

Zoe Goodall, aged 12

Darren drank dirty drain water.

Victoria Newton, aged 12

Red lorry, yellow lorry.

Anon

Cricket critic.

Anon

A tutor who tooted the flute
Tried to tutor two tooters to toot.
  Said the two to the tutor,
  'Is it harder to toot, or
To tutor two tooters to toot?'

Carolyn Wells

One old Oxford ox opening oysters;
Two tee-totums totally tired of trying to trot to Tadbury;
Three tall tigers tippling tenpenny tea;
Four fat friars fanning fainting flies;
Five frippy Frenchmen foolishly fishing for flies;
Six sportsmen shooting snipes;
Seven Severn salmons swallowing shrimps;
Eight Englishmen eagerly examining Europe;
Nine nimble noblemen nibbling nonpareils;
Ten tinkers tinkling upon ten tin tinder-boxes with ten tenpenny tacks;
Eleven elephants elegantly equipt;
Twelve typographical topographers typically translating types.

Anon

DISCUSSION

Alliteration is often used in tongue-twisters, but it is not the only thing that makes them so difficult to say. As you try these examples, listen carefully for the exact place where you go wrong, and discuss what causes the problem.

WRITING

Write a first name tongue-twister based on the names in your class. Group them together so that they are as difficult as possible to say.

Write tongue-twisters based on:

  place names
  school subjects
  favourite foods

Read through the tongue-twisters in this chapter looking for the combinations of letters which are trickiest to say. Make up your own tongue-twisters based on these letters.

Poetry Puzzle

Read these 'phonetic poems' and try to answer the questions below.

PHONETIC POEM   **PHONETIC POEM, 1924**

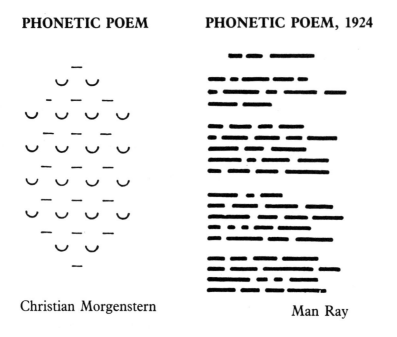

Christian Morgenstern   Man Ray

Are these really poems? How are they like poems?

How many verses are there in the second poem?

What are the poems about?

What important feature of ordinary poems do they lack?

Were they written to get people thinking about the nature of poetry, or simply as a joke? What aspect of poetry do they emphasise?

Add words to Man Ray's poem. Try to make the length of the word similar to the length of the dash.

Write (or draw!) your own phonetic poems.

12
Speak Out!

If poetry sometimes seems to be too remote and abstract, one of the reasons may be that we read silently and alone words that were meant to be heard aloud by an audience, and the life has gone out of it. Except for the last hundred years or so, most poetry was recited rather than read—and this is still so in many parts of the world. Much of the poetry in this book is better read out loud. Spells, for example, are only effective when spoken. Epics, like *Beowulf*, and ballads were designed to be recited and the humorous poetry, like all humour, is more enjoyable when shared. In this chapter is a selection of poetry which is particularly effective when read aloud. Working in pairs or small groups, divide the poems into parts and take it in turns to perform one to your class.

This traditional pygmy poem is a celebration of the living world through words and actions. The reader of the solo parts should try to move like the animal being described.

Song of the Animal World

Solo:	The fish goes . . .	*Chorus:*	Hip!
	The bird goes . . .		Viss!
	The monkey goes . . .		Gnan!

Solo: (with actions)
I jump to the left,
I turn to the right,
I'm being the fish
That slips through the water, that slips,
That twists and springs!

Everything lives, everything dances, everything chirps . . .

   The fish . . .   Hip!

   The bird . . .   Viss!

   The monkey . . .   Gnan!

Solo: (with actions)

   The bird flies away,

   Flies, flies, flies,

   Goes, comes back, passes,

   Rises, floats, swoops,

   I'm being the bird.

Everything lives, everything dances, everything chirps . . .

   The fish . . .   Hip!

   The bird . . .   Viss!

   The monkey . . .   Gnan!

Solo: (with actions)

   The monkey—from branch to branch

   He runs, hops, jumps,

   With his wife and his brat,

   His mouth stuffed full, his tail in the air.

   Here's the monkey, here's the monkey!

Everything lives, everything dances, everything chirps . . .

   The fish . . .   Hip!

   The bird . . .   Viss!

   The monkey . . .   Gnan!

                Traditional Pygmy

Oo-oo-ah-ah!

A woman in a churchyard sat,

 Oo-oo-ah-ah!

Very short and very fat,

 Oo-oo-ah-ah!

She saw three corpses carried in,

 Oo-oo-ah-ah!

Very tall and very thin,

 Oo-oo-ah-ah!

Woman to the corpses said,
  Oo-oo-ah-ah!

Corpses to the woman said,
  Oo-oo-ah-ah!
Yes, you'll be like us when you are dead,
  Oo-oo-ah-ah!
Woman to the corpses said—
                    (Silence)

                              Anon

Overheard on a Saltmarsh

Nymph, nymph, what are your beads?
Green glass, goblin. Why do you stare at them?
Give them me.
                    No.
Give them me. Give them me.
                    No.
Then I will howl all night in the reeds,
Lie in the mud and howl for them.

Goblin, why do you love them so?
They are better than stars or water,
Better than voices of winds that sing,
Better than any man's fair daughter,
Your green glass beads on a silver ring.

Hush I stole them out of the moon.

Give me your beads, I desire them.
                    No.

I will howl in a deep lagoon
For your green glass beads, I love them so.
Give them me. Give them.
              No.

                         Harold Monro

'Blackened-Face' Dirge-Proper for Atiroa

[Solo]   Alas, Pangeivi! The case is hopeless.
        The canoe is lost;

[Chorus] Oh, my god Tane thou hast failed me!
        Thou didst promise life;
        Thy worshippers were to be as a forest,
        To fall only by the axe in battle.
        Had it been the god Turanga—
        That liar! I would not have trusted him.
        Like him, you are a man-eater!
        May thy mouth be covered with dung;
        Slush it over and over!
        This god is but a man after all!

[Solo]   Plaster him well, friends. Ha! Ha!

[Chorus] Dung is fit food for such gods!
        We parents are in deep mourning,
        Like that first used by Tiki.
        We mourn for our beloved first-born.
        Oh, that one could stir up the gods,
        And cause the very dead to awake!
        Yonder stands thy weeping mother.
        Thy spirit wanders about One-makenukenu,
        Inquiring the reason
        Why his poor body was devoured by the gods.
        Fairy of the axe! cleave open
        The secret road to spirit-land; and
        Compel Vatea to give up the dead!

[Solo]   Fart, Tiki, a fart such as only ghosts can!

[Chorus] Wait a moment.

[Solo]   Fart, fart away!
        (Chorus of pretended farts)

[Chorus] A curse upon thee, priest Pangeivi.
        Thou hast destroyed my boy.

                      Polynesia

The Feckless Dinner Party

'Who are we waiting for?' 'Soup burnt?' . . . Eight—
   'Only the tiniest party.—Us!'
'Darling! Divine!' 'Ten minutes late—
   'And my digest—' 'I'm ravenous!'

' "Toomes"?'—'Oh, he's new.' 'Looks crazed, I guess.'
   ' "Married"—Again!' 'Well; more or less!'

'Dinner is served!' ' "Dinner is served"!'
   'Is served?' 'Is served.' 'Ah, yes.'

'Dear Mr Prout, will you take down
   The Lilith in leaf-green by the fire?
Blanche Ogleton? . . .' 'How coy a frown!—
   Hasn't she borrowed Eve's attire?'
'Morose Old Adam!' 'Charmed—I vow.'
   'Come then, and meet her now.'

'Now, Dr Mallus—would you please?—
   Our daring poetess, Delia Seek?'
'The lady with the bony knees?'
   'And—*entre nous*—less song than beak.'
'Sharing her past with Simple Si—'
   'Bare facts! He'll blush!' 'Oh, fie!'

'And you, Sir Nathan—false but fair!—
   That fountain of wit, Aurora Pert.'
'More wit than It, poor dear! But there . . .'
   'Pitiless Pasha! And such a flirt!'
' "Flirt"! Me?' 'Who else?' 'You here . . . Who can . . .?'
   'Incorrigible man!'

'And now, Mr Simon—Little me!—
   Last and—' 'By no means least!' 'Oh, come!
What naughty, naughty flattery!
   Honey!—I hear the creature hum!'
'Sweets for the sweet, I always say!'
   ' "Always"? . . . We're last.' 'This way?' . . .

'No, sir; straight on, please.' 'I'd have vowed!—
    I came the other . . .' 'It's queer; I'm sure . . .'
'What frightful pictures!' 'Fiends!' 'The crowd!'
    'Such news!' 'I can't endure . . .'

'Yes, there they go.' 'Heavens! Are we right!'
    'Follow up closer!' ' "Prout"?—sand-blind!'
'This endless . . .' 'Who's turned down the light?'
    'Keep calm! They're close behind.'

'Oh! Dr Mallus; what dismal stairs!'
    'I hate these old Victor . . .' 'Dry rot!'
'Darker and darker!' 'Fog!' 'The air's . . .'
    'Scarce breathable!' 'Hell!' 'What?'

'The banister's gone!' 'It's deep; keep close!'
    'We're going down and down!' 'What fun!'
'Damp! Why, my shoes . . .' 'It's slimy . . . Not *moss*!'
    'I'm freezing cold!' 'Let's run.'

'. . . Behind us. I'm giddy . . .' 'The catacombs . . .'
    'That shout!' 'Who's there?' 'I'm *alone*!' 'Stand back!'
'She said, Lead . . .' 'Oh!' 'Where's Toomes?' '*Toomes*!'
    'TOOMES!'
    'Stifling!' 'My skull will crack!'

'Sir Nathan! Ai!' 'I say! *Toomes*! Prout!'
    'Where? Where?' ' "Our silks and fine array" . . .'
'She's mad.' 'I'm dying!' 'Oh, let me *out*!'
    'My God! We've lost our way!' . . .

And now how sad-serene the abandoned house,
Whereon at dawn the spring-tide sunbeams beat;
And time's slow pace alone is ominous,
And naught but shadows of noonday therein meet;
Domestic microcosm, only a Trump could rouse:
And, pondering darkly, in the silent rooms,
He who misled them all—the butler, Toomes.

Walter de la Mare

Poetry Puzzle

Read this poem aloud to some friends and ask them to guess what illness you are suffering from.

Belagcholly Days

Chilly Dovebber with his boadigg blast
   Dow cubs add strips the bedow add the lawd,
Eved October's suddy days are past—
   Add Subber's gawd!

I kdow dot what it is to which I cligg
   That stirs to sogg add sorrow, yet I trust
That still I sigg, but as the liddets sigg—
   Because I bust.

Add now, farewell to roses add to birds,
   To larded fields and tigkligg streablets eke;
Farewell to all articulated words
   I fain would speak.

Farewell, by cherished strolliggs od the sward,
   Greed glades and forest shades, farewell to you;
With sorrowing heart I, wretched add forlord,
   Bid you—achew!!!

Anon

How did the writer get the effect of a person with a cold?

Can you understand every word in the poem? Read it again, but this time imagine your cold has gone. What word are you going to put in place of the sneeze at the end of the poem (clue—it sounds very similar!)

Which sounds are particularly affected by a person with a cold? Why?

Now try writing some of your own 'cold' poems.

13
Wordplay

Knock, knock,
'Who's there?'
'Olive.'
'Olive who?'
'Olive here, so let me in!'

Knock, knock,
'Who's there?'
'Tick.'
'Tick who?'
'Tick 'em up, I'm a tongue-tied cowboy.'

Knock, knock,
'Who's there?'
'Frank.'
'Frank who?'
'Frankenstein.'

Knock, knock,
'Who's there?'
'Wilma.'
'Wilma who?'
'Wilma supper be ready soon?'

You may be wondering what 'Knock, knock' jokes are doing in a book on poetry. We have already seen that some jokes are a kind of free verse poetry because the words are arranged in some kind of pattern. These 'Knock, knock' jokes have a very clear pattern. They also share another important technique with poetry—*wordplay*. Wordplay is playing around with the sound and sense of words just for the fun of it! The commonest type of wordplay, used in jokes, advertising and many other kinds of writing, is the *pun*. A pun is a play upon words with a double meaning—any slight alteration of sound or spelling necessary to make the pun work is all part of the fun:

Knock, knock,
'Who's there?'
'Arfer.'
'Arfer who?'
'Arfer got.'

Puns are used in exactly the same way in poetry:

Radi was a circus lion,
Radi was a woman hater,
Radi had a lady trainer,
Radiator.

The pun in the last line is a play on the real meaning 'Radi ate her' and the word 'radiator', which has nothing to do with the subject of the poem and results in a ridiculous and humorous clash of ideas. In many puns of this kind there is a choice of spelling—sometimes the wrong choice will spoil the effect.

Now read and enjoy the following poems, and keep on the alert for examples of wordplay:

A little girl opened the door to her teacher.
'Are your parents in?' asked the teacher.
'They was in,' said the little girl,
'but they is out now.'
'They WAS in! They IS out!' exclaimed the teacher.
'Where is your grammar?'
'In the front room watching the telly.'

                                   Anon

Things You Never Saw

A shoe box
A salad bowl
A square dance

                    Anon

Stately Verse

If Mary goes far out to sea,
By wayward breezes fanned,
I'd like to know—can you tell me?—
Just where would Maryland?

If Tenny went high up in air
And looked o'er land and lea,
Looked here and there and everywhere,
Pray what would Tennessee?

I looked out of the window and
Saw Orry on the lawn;
He's not there now, and who can tell
Just where has Oregon?

Two girls were quarrelling one day
With garden tools, and so
I said, 'My dears, let Mary rake
And just let Idaho.'

A friend of mine lived in a flat
With half a dozen boys;
When he fell ill I asked him why.
He said: 'I'm Illinois.'

An English lady had a steed.
She called him 'Ighland Bay.
She rode for exercise, and thus
Rhode Island every day.

Anon

Teacher: 'Which one of you can use "fascinate" in a proper sentence?'
Jimmy: 'Please teacher, I can.'
Teacher: 'All right, Jimmy, go ahead.'
Jimmy: 'My raincoat has ten buttons on it but I can only fasten eight.'

Anon

GRUESOME

I was sitting in the sitting room
toying with some toys
when from a door marked 'GRUESOME'
there came a GRUESOME noise.

Cautiously I opened it
and there to my surprise
a little GRUE lay sitting
with tears in its eyes

'Oh little GRUE please tell me
what is it ails thee so?'
'Well I'm so small,' he sobbed,
'GRUESSES don't want to know.'

'Exercises are the answer,
Each morning you must DO SOME.'
He thanked me, smiled,
and do you know what?
The very next day he . . .

Roger McGough

A Goblin Funeral Director

I'm a Goblin Mortician,
That's why I'm wearing black,
I drive 'em off to the graveyard
But I never bring 'em back.

People are quite tearful
When relatives end their day
But honestly, it cheers me up
To see 'em drive away.

And now I give the reason
I say it with misgiving;
To some people what they call death
I will call a living.

Spike Milligan

Vampires

I hate vampires
They're old
They're ugly
They smell rotten.

I hate vampires
They're mean
They're cruel
They're a pain in the neck!

Brian Loutfi, aged 13

Stop Spooking!

A little spook
Went to spook school
To learn how to be spooky
But he was so noisy
That his spooky teacher said
'Don't spook until you're spooken to!'

Simon Weston, aged 13

Riddle

What a hideous cackling and whistling
Interrupt my sleep!
I open the curtains. What do I see and hear? . . .
Two brooms brushing the tree-tops,
Two cloaks blowing in the wind,
Two cats holding tight,
Two jockeys shouting,
'I'll beat you to the moon! I'll beat you to the moon!'

I wonder *which* will win.

Ian Serraillier

THINGS TO DO

Exchange some 'Knock, knock' jokes with your friends and make a collection of the best ones. Take care with the setting out and punctuation and it will have the added bonus of giving you some practice in writing direct speech.

Explain the title 'Stately Verse'. Write out the last line of each verse in a way that brings out the *other* meaning. What would the poem lose if it had been printed this way?

What two words are missing from the last line of 'Gruesome'?

What does Ian Serraillier's riddle describe? A clue is given in the form of a pun.

Explain the two different meanings in each line of 'Things You Never Saw'. Read each line twice trying to bring out the different meanings. What differences of tone or emphasis did you notice? Copy out the poem and try to add a few more lines.

Write some short pun poems of your own. A good way to do this is to take a simple joke based on a pun and expand it into a poem, as Brian Loutfi and Simon Weston have done (it might also be worth referring back to the work you did on jokes and poems in Chapter Two).

Keep your eyes open for puns used in advertisements, and newspaper headlines and captions. Make a class collection of these for display.

Lear's Riddles

What saint should be the patron of Malta?

Saint Sea-bastian.

And why are the kisses of mermaids pleasant at breakfast?

Because they are a kind of Water Caresses.

When may the Lanes and Roads have shed tears of sympathy?

When the Street' SWEPT.

What letter confounds Comets and Cookery?

G—for it turns Astronomy into Gastronomy.

Why are beginners on a Pianoforte like parasites on the backs of deceased fishes?

Because they are always running up and down their damned scales.

Why could not Eve have the measles?

Because she'd ADAM.

Edward Lear

This kind of joke can be heard almost every day among school pupils, so you may be surprised to hear that these examples were written about a hundred years ago by the nonsense poet, Edward Lear. Like the 'Knock, knock' jokes which we looked at in the last chapter, they depend on puns for their humour.

You probably know many more jokes of this kind. Make a collection of them and try making up some of your own.

14
Vogon Poetry and Other Nonsense

If you have been disappointed with your attempts at poetry so far, don't worry—it can't be as bad as Vogon poetry, as you will see from reading this extract from *The Hitchhiker's Guide to the Galaxy*! Vogon Jeltz' excruciatingly bad poem will renew your confidence, as well as providing an introduction to nonsense poetry.

Vogon poetry is of course the third worst in the Universe. The second worse is that of the Azgoths of Kria. During a recitation by their Poet Master Grunthos the Flatulent of his poem 'Ode To A Small Lump of Green Putty I Found In My Armpit One Midsummer Morning' four of his audience died of internal haemorrhaging, and the President of the Mid-Galactic Arts Nobbling Council survived by gnawing one of his own legs off. Grunthos is reported to have been 'disappointed' by the poem's reception, and was about to embark on a reading of his twelve-book epic entitled *My Favourite Bathtime Gurgles* when his own major intestine, in a desperate attempt to save life and civilization, leapt straight up through his neck and throttled his brain.

The very worst poetry of all perished along with its creator Paula Nancy Millstone Jennings of Greenbridge, Essex, England in the destruction of the planet Earth.

Prostetnic Vogon Jeltz smiled very slowly. This was done not so much for effect as because he was trying to remember the sequence of muscle movements. He had had a terribly therapeutic yell at his prisoners and was now feeling quite relaxed and ready for a little callousness.

The prisoners sat in Poetry Appreciation chairs—strapped in. Vogons suffered no illusions as to the regard their works were generally held in. Their early attempts at composition had been part of a bludgeoning insistence that they be accepted as a properly evolved and cultured race, but now the only thing that kept them going was sheer bloodymindedness.

The sweat stood out cold on Ford Prefect's brow, and slid round the electrodes strapped to his temples. These were attached to a battery of electronic equipment—imagery intensifiers, rhythmic modulators, alliterative residulators and simile dumpers—all designed to heighten the experience of the poem and make sure that not a single nuance of the poet's thought was lost.

Arthur Dent sat and quivered. He had no idea what he was in for, but he knew that he hadn't liked anything that had happened so far and didn't think things were likely to change.

The Vogon began to read—a fetid little passage of his own devising. 'Oh freddled gruntbuggly . . .' he began. Spasms wracked Ford's body—this was worse than even he'd been prepared for.

'. . . thy micturations are to me / As plurdled gabbleblotchits on a lurgid bee.'

'Aaaaaaaaaaaargggggggggghhhhhhhhh!' went Ford Prefect, wrenching his head back as lumps of pain thumped through it. He could dimly see beside him Arthur lolling and rolling in his seat. He clenched his teeth. 'Groop I implore thee,' continued the merciless Vogon, 'My foonting turlingdromes.'

His voice was rising to a horrible pitch of impassioned stridency, 'And hooptiously drangle me with crinkly bindlewurdles, / Or I will rend thee in the gobberwarts with my blurglecruncheon, see if I don't!'

'Nnnnnnnnnnnnyyyyyyyyyyyyuuuuuuuuuuuurrrrrrrrrrrgggggggggggghhhhhhhhhhh!' cried Ford Prefect and threw one final spasm as the electronic enhancement of the last line caught him full blast across the temples. He went limp. Arthur lolled.

THINGS TO DO

Write a poem of the kind that might have been written by Paula Nancy Millstone Jennings of Greenbridge, Essex.

With careful reference to the passage, draw a detailed diagram of a poetry appreciation chair.

Most of Vogon Jeltz' poem is given in this extract. Using what is given, complete the poem and give it a title (note that a diagonal stroke, /, means begin a new line). Try to add at least another ten lines to finish it off.

Write a translation into clear English (you will have to use a lot of guesswork and imagination).

OTHER NONSENSE

There is just enough recognisable English in Vogon Jeltz' poem to make an answer to the last question possible. This is because the nonsense words are made up of bits of English mixed together—wordplay gone mad! Here are some examples of different types of nonsense poetry. Some, like Vogon Jeltz' poem, are written with nonsense words, others are written in ordinary English but the meaning is nonsense.

Away from It All

I wish I were a Tibetan monk
Living in a monastery.
I would unpack my trunk
And store it in a tronastery;
I would collect all my junk
And send it to a jonastery;
I would try to reform a drunk,
And pay his expenses at a dronastery.
If my income shrunk
I would send it to a shronastery.

Ogden Nash

O'er Seas That Have No Beaches

O'er seas that have no beaches
To end their waves upon,
I floated with twelve peaches,
A sofa and a swan.

The blunt waves crashed above us
The sharp waves burst around,
There was no one to love us,
No hope of being found—

Where, on the notched horizon
So endlessly a-drip,
I saw all of a sudden
No sign of any ship.

Mervyn Peake

There were three ghostesses
Sitting on postesses
Eating buttered toastesses
And greasing their fistesses
Right up to their wristesses,
Weren't they beastesses
To make such feastesses!

Anon

Little Spider

Little Spider
spider sadly
in the webly
light of leaves!
Why deride a
spide's mentadly
when it's hebly
full of grieves?

Little spider
legged and lonely
in the bony
way of thieves.
Where's the fly-da
on the phonebly?

Mervyn Peake

I am writing these lines
From inside a lion,
And it's rather dark in here,
So please excuse the handwriting
Which may not be too clear.
But this afternoon by the lion's cage
I'm afraid I got too near.
And I'm writing these lines
From inside a lion,
And it's rather dark in here.

Shen Silverstein

The ankle's chief end is exposiery
Of the latest designs in silk hosiery;
   Also, I suspect,
   It's a means to connect
The part called the calf with the toesiery.

Anon

Lorenzo dwelt at Heighington,
  (Hys cote was made of Dimity,)
Least-ways yf not exactly there,
  Yet yn yts close proximity.
Hee called on mee—hee stayed to tee—
  Yet not a word hee ut-tered,
Untyl I sayd, 'D'ye lyke your bread
Dry?' and hee answered 'But-tered.'
  (*Chorus*) Noodle dumb
        Has a noodle-head,
I hate such noodles, *I* do.

Lewis Carroll

Chuffa-luffa steam train,
Chuggle up the track,
Chuggle up to Nowhere,
Chuggle-chuffle back.

Ever been to Nowhere?
No—what's there?
Nothing.
Nothing?
Nothing but a steam train,

Chuggle up the track,
Chuggle up to Nowhere,
Chuggle-chuffle back.

Peter Wesley-Smith

Marezle toats,
Dozle toats,
Dozle tivy-too.

Anon

A Letter to Evelyn Baring

Thrippsy pillivinx,
  Inky tinky pobbleboskle abblesquabs?—
Flosky! beebul trimble flosky!—Okul
scratchabibblebongibo, viddle squibble tog-a-tog,
ferrymoyassity amsky flamsky ramsky damsky
crocklefether squiggs.
         Flinkywisty pomm,
         Slushypipp.

Edward Lear

EXERCISES

Add some more lines to 'Away from It All'. For example, where would a *punk* live?

In 'Little Spider' which nonsense words have been suggested by the words 'spider' and 'sadly'? How do you think the word 'grieves' was formed? What does it mean?

Try to translate the poem into plain English.

Lewis Carroll has made some slight changes in spelling to suggest medieval English. What are they? Why are 'ut-tered' and 'But-tered' spelt with a hyphen in the middle? Write your own 'medieval' nonsense poem.

'A Letter to Evelyn Baring' and 'Marezle Toats' are the ultimate in nonsense—neither the words nor the meaning make sense. Is there any point in writing poems like this? Did you enjoy them? In what way? Write some of your own.

'Chuffa-luffa' and 'chuggle' are nonsense words which have been invented to convey the sound of a steam train. Write some short poems to suggest the sounds of a ticking clock, a police car and a pneumatic drill.

'O'er Seas That Have No Beaches' owes some of its nonsensical humour to the unlikely collection of objects brought together in the first verse. What are these objects and why is it unlikely that they would be found together? What else in the poem is ridiculous, unlikely or contradictory?

Dream up ridiculous combinations of objects, then write poems or short stories about them. Here's a list to start you off (notice that some of the objects are linked by alliteration):

   a ghost   a guitar   an alarm clock   a toadstool   a typewriter

Give your friend a ridiculous combination of objects to write a poem about—make it as difficult as possible.

A Riddle Poem

Each verse of this poem is a riddle describing a mammal or a reptile. How many can you guess?

> A handsome beast and rather shy
> It sounds a very costly buy.
>
> Put together bit by bit
> An insect and a moonlight flit.
>
> At sport he's only a beginner
> But cooked he makes a tasty dinner.
>
> What's that coming from above?
> It's water from the clouds my love.
>
> He's not intentionally rude
> Although it sounds as if he's nude.
>
> We're told we know what sailors are
> Well, here's a very backward tar.
>
> He may be black or brown or brindle
> And works a very crafty swindle.
>
> He likes the hot and sunny weather
> For putting two + two together.
>
> An ugly spot may well be found
> Travelling by underground.
>
> This river dweller would inform a
> Cockney that it's getting warmer.
>
> It sounds as if this creature's plight is
> Suffering from laryngitis.
>
> A creature judging by the sound
> With which the human head is crowned.
>
> Some are small and some are whoppers
> A form of transport used by coppers.
>
> You'll find him at the London Zoo
> He's black and white and walked on too.

Add more verses to the poem.

15
Atmosphere

The night-wind rattles the window-frame—
I wake up shivering, shivering, all alone.
Darkness. Silence. What's the time?
Mother's asleep, and Dad's not home.
Shivering in the corner, shivering all alone.

Who's there—standing behind the curtain?
Shivering in the corner, no need to cry . . .
It's only the shadow of the tree in the garden
Shaking and sighing as the wind rushes by.
Shivering in the corner, and no need to cry.

Brian Lee

What is the child in the poem frightened of? There is no one else in the room—no ghost or burgler, no one 'standing behind the curtain.' He is frightened by the eerie atmosphere of his room late at night, created by the darkness and the noise of the wind rattling the window-frame. Atmosphere is very important to a horror poem—the right atmosphere can make even the most ordinary things seem sinister, yet without it even the most gruesome catalogue of horrors wouldn't so much as raise a shudder.

The best way to learn how to create atmosphere is to study how the experts do it. Begin by reading these examples:

The Haunted House

On a hilltop bleak and bare
looms the castle of despair,
only phantoms linger there
within its dismal walls.
Through the dark they're creeping, crawling,
frenzied furies battling, brawling,
sprawling, calling, caterwauling
through the dusky halls.

Filmy visions, ever flocking,
dart through chambers, crudely-mocking,
rudely rapping, tapping, knocking
on the crumbling doors.
Tortured spirits whine and wail,
they grope and grasp, they wildly flail,
their hollow voices rasp and rail
beneath the moldering floors.

                              Jack Prelutsky

The Queer Moment

It was a queer moment when all on my own
    I woke up in the gloom
To hear, far away, the bell of a church
    Go *boom, boom, boom.*

It was a queer minute when something in the walls
    Scampered and scampered, on and on,
And the wind whimpered about the house
    Please, please let me in . . .

It was a queer hour as I listened to the clock
    Tick-tock, fidget on the wall,
And my breath wouldn't come, and my heart knock-knocked
    For no reason at all.

                              Brian Lee

90

Matthew Gates, aged 14

The Silent Spinney

What's that rustling behind me?
Only a cat.
Thank goodness for that,
For I'm afraid of the darkness,
And these tall trees
Are silent and black,
And if ever I get out of here, mate,
I can tell you I'm not coming back.

There's a dark shadow out in the roadway,
See if there's someone behind that tree,
For I'm afraid of the darkness
And it might jump out at me.

My sisters are scared stiff of spiders,
My mother is frightened of mice,
But I'm afraid of the darkness,
I'm not coming this way twice.

                              Seamus Redmond

Spellbound

The night is darkening round me,
The wild winds coldly blow;
But a tyrant spell has bound me
And I cannot, cannot go.

The giant trees are bending
Their bare boughs weighed with snow.
And the storm is fast descending,
And yet I cannot go.

Clouds beyond clouds above me,
Wastes beyond wastes below;
But nothing drear can move me;
I will not, cannot go.

                              Emily Bronte

Church and Churchyard at Night

See yonder hallowed church! the pious work
Of names once famed, now dubious or forgot
And buried midst the wreck of things which were:
There lie interr'd the more illustrious dead.
The wind is up. Hark how it howls! Methinks
Till now I never heard a sound so dreary.
Doors creak and windows clap, and night's foul bird
Rooked in the spire screams loud. The gloomy aisles
Black-plastered and hung round with shreds of scutcheons
And tattered coats of arms, send back the sound
Laden with heavier airs, from the low vaults
The mansions of the dead. Roused from their slumbers
In grim array the grizzly spectres rise,
Grin horrible, and obstinately sullen
Pass and repass, hushed as the foot of night.
Again the screech-owl shrieks! Ungracious sound!
I'll hear no more, it makes one's blood run chill.

    Quite round the pile, a row of reverend elms,
Coeval near with that, all ragged show,
Long lashed by the rude winds. Some rift half down
Their branchless trunks, others so thin a top

That scarce two crows could lodge in the same tree.
Strange things, the neighbours say, have happened here.
Wild shrieks have issued from the hollow tombs,
Dead men have come again, and walked about,
And the great bell has tolled, unrung, untouched.
(Such tales they tell at wake or gossiping,
When it draws near to witching time of night.)
    Oft, in the lone churchyard at night I've seen
By glimpse of moonshine, chequering through the trees,
The schoolboy with his satchel in his hand,
Whistling aloud to bear his courage up,
And lightly tripping o'er the long flat stones
(With nettles skirted and with moss o'ergrown),
That tell in homely phrase who lie below.
Sudden he starts and hears, or thinks he hears
The sound of something purring at his heels.
Full fast he flies, and dares not look behind him,
Till out of breath he overtakes his fellows,
Who gather round, and wonder at the tale
Of horrid apparition, tall and ghastly,
That walks at dead of night, or takes his stand
O'er some new-opened grave—and strange to tell,
Vanishes at crowing of the cock!

Robert Blair

from **The Last Tryst**

Ink-black clouds banked in the north-east:
The force of the coming storm latent in the forest,
    Waiting as quietly as the bats hanging
  In the branches. Darkness blanketing
    Dense leaves that are still and silent
    As a crouching tiger intent
      On its prey. Flocks of crows
  Suddenly aloft in a craze
      Of fear, like tattered
      Shreds of darkness littered
    Over the void of a cosmos
    Broken into chaos.

Rabindranath Tagore

Nightmare!

Alone,
In a room
Surrounded by light,
A light with no source.

Running, escaping,
From what?
Nothing is there
But I still feel the fear.

My legs are lead weights
And the floor is covered in glue.
It is a magnet
For I seem hardly able to move.

I am running down a corridor
Full of a thousand faces,
They are huge and distorted
They scream at me.

Then,
Nothing, I am now alone, screaming.
What is my horror?
I do not know.

But still, the reality remains,
Imprinted on my mind,
And still, the cold sweat remains,
Imprinted on my pillow.

Andrew Jeckells, aged 12

EXERCISES

Each poet has created a different atmosphere. Try briefly to describe the atmosphere of each poem. These words will help you:

anxiety   desolation   dread   eeriness   fear
horror   mystery   panic   suspense   gloom

Working in pairs, take each poem in turn and discuss how the poet has created an atmosphere. Here's how to go about it:

> Jot down any mention of sounds, or the effects of light—for example, 'doors creak and windows clap', 'moonshine chequering through the trees'.
> Jot down any descriptive details that catch your imagination—for example, 'the grizzly spectres rise/Grin horrible . . .'
> Jot down hints about people's feelings—for example, 'shivering in the corner—no need to cry.'

Discuss the words and phrases you have picked out and try to explain why they are effective, then write a short piece about the poem you liked best, explaining how the poet created an atmosphere to suit the subject.

WRITING

Choose a subject from the list given below and imagine it as clearly as you can. (The key to creating atmosphere—and all vivid writing—is your imagination.) Write down your ideas as quickly as possible—while they are fresh in your mind—you can worry about technical details later. Finally, shape your ideas into a poem in free or rhymed verse, using where appropriate any of the techniques you have learned so far.

Suggested titles:

Crumbling Crookhill Hall
Monks and bones
The shadowy moon
Bad dreams
Alone—at night!
A short cut through the churchyard
Was it an owl, or . . .?
Things that go 'bump' in the night

Poetry Puzzle

Here is another riddle which has been made by omitting the title from a poem. What is the subject of the poem, and what was the title?

> Blood is an acquired taste
> 'tis warm and sickly
> and sticks to the teeth
> a surfeit makes me puke.
> I judge my victims as a connoisseur
> a sip here, a mouthful there.
> I never kill
> and am careful to cause no pain
> to those who sleeping nourish me
> and calling once I never call again.
>
> So if one morning you awake,
> stretch, and remember
> dark dreams of
>   falling
>   falling
> if your neck is sore
> a mark that wasn't there the night before
> be not afeared 'tis but a sign
> i give thee thanks
> i have drunk thy wine.
>
>   Roger McGough

A RIDDLING COMPETITION

Write some riddles of your own based on the different types of riddles covered in this book. The idea is to take it in turns to solve each other's riddles. An exciting example of this can be found in Chapter Five of *The Hobbit* by J. R. R. Tolkien in which Bilbo has a life-or-death riddling competition with an evil creature called Gollum.

16
Description

The way to describe something vividly is to imagine it vividly—the words will then come automatically. This process can be helped by making a conscious effort to learn and use a wider range of descriptive words. Below is a list of describing words (*adjectives*) for you to complete and use. Letters A–E have been done already to give you the idea. The best way to complete this list is to browse through a dictionary and jot down all the words that you think will help your descriptions. To save time you could work in small groups dividing the letters of the alphabet between you. When you have finished make a neat copy of your list.

abhorrent	bloodthirsty
abominable	chill
abysmal	creaking
agonising	creeping
ancient	enchanted
antiquated	evil
bleak	evil-smelling
bone-chilling	excruciating
blood-curdling	extraordinary
blood-sucking	

These adjectives should be seen only as a starting-point—there are thousands more! Looking up these words in a thesaurus will suggest many more possibilities. You will also come across good descriptive words when you are reading poems—you could add them to your list.

You will find the list a useful reference when you are writing horror poems or stories. Simply browsing through it could give you an idea. One word of warning though—make sure you know the meaning of a word before you use it. Look it up in a dictionary if you are at all uncertain.

ADJECTIVE POEMS

These poems will give you some practice in using your list. They consist of four to eight lines of free verse, with two adjectives and one noun in each line. Fill in the gaps with adjectives from the list, a thesaurus, or your own vocabulary, and then write some of your own.

Ancient, evil-smelling crypt,
Huge, black coffin,
——————, —————— vampire,
Beautiful, sleeping girl,
Open, unguarded window,
——————, —————— teeth,
——————, —————— blood,
Satisfied, sleeping vampire.

Tired, dispirited traveller,
Lashing, driving rain,
Dry, deserted house.
——————, —————— noise,
——————, —————— shadow,
——————, —————— ghost!

Foolish, ghost-hunting children,
——————, —————— night,
——————, —————— churchyard,
——————, —————— shadow,
Cloaked, monkish figure,
——————, frightened children,
Frantic, —————— escape,
Puzzled, bewildered vicar.

Look at this picture and discuss how you would describe it. Don't forget to consult your word list and a thesaurus for ideas. Jot down any words or phrases which you think are particularly effective and use them to write a poem about the picture.

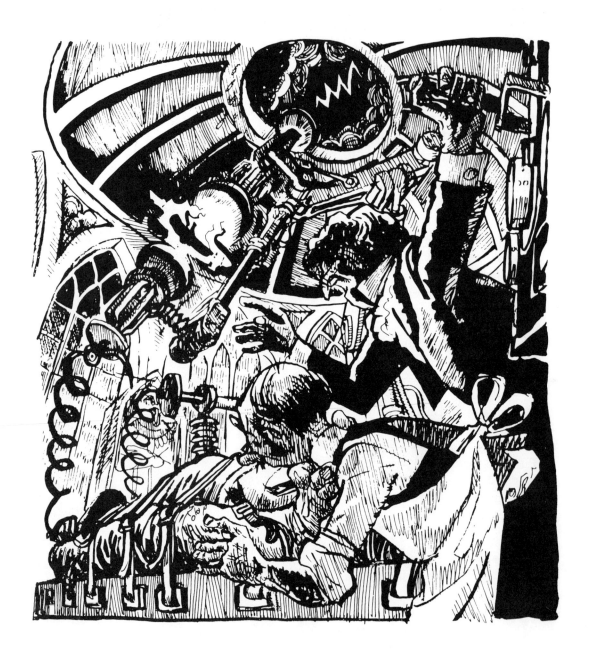

Barry Brooks, aged 14

17
Shades of Meaning

A ghost has just walked into the room! You are *frightened* and your friend is *terrified*. Who is most afraid?

Frightened and *terrified* both have similar meanings (words which have similar meanings are called *synonyms*). Both words express a feeling of fear and yet they don't mean exactly the same: they have different shades of meaning—*terrified* is more intense than *frightened*.

Here is another example. The first sentence on this page uses the word *ghost*, but any of the synonyms—apparition, phantom, shade, spectre, spook—could have been used. The meanings are practically the same. However, if *spook* had been used you would probably have expected something humorous to follow, because this is a 'joke' word for ghost. Even when there is very little, if any, difference in *meaning*, as in apparition, phantom, spectre, there is a difference in *sound* which may be important for rhyme, rhythm (you may need a word with a certain number of syllables to fit the rhythm of your poem) or alliteration. These differences are sometimes so subtle that dictionaries don't attempt to explain them—you have to rely on your intuition.

It is important in all your writing that you try to think of the word which has exactly the shade of meaning you want (rather than writing the first word which comes into your head). This is particularly so in poetry, when you will need to consider subtleties of sound as well as subtleties of meaning.

A valuable tool in the quest for the right word is a thesaurus. If you have an idea and can't think of a word for it, look up the nearest word you can think of and it will give you (or refer you to) a list of words of similar meaning, among which may be the word you want. Use a thesaurus regularly and it will help to widen your vocabulary.

EXERCISES

Discuss the different shades of meaning in the following words, which are all synonyms of *smell*:

    aroma   odour   perfume   pong   scent   stench   stink

Which would you use in the following sentences, and why?

> The atmosphere in the crypt was choking because of the ——————— of rotting corpses.
>
> Freshly ground coffee has a delightful ———————.
>
> Pooh! Your feet ———————!

Make up appropriate sentences for the words you have not used.

Discuss any differences in meaning or sound in this group of words. Try to arrange them in order, from the mildest to the strongest form of surprise.

    amazed   astounded   astonished   surprised

Which word would you use in this couplet, and why?

> Timothy was quite ———————
> To see how bright his bonfire blazed.

Do the same with these words:

    awful   dreadful   frightful   grim   gruesome   hideous   terrible

Which would you use in this couplet, and why?

> The ——————— ghoul dug up the ground—
> I dare not tell you what he found!

Read through this poem carefully considering the synonyms given. Choose the words which you think have exactly the right shade of meaning and quality of sound, and write out your version of the poem.

A	spook	creeps			
	ghost	flits		black	darkness
	phantom	floats	through the	ghostly	gloom
	shade	glides		gloomy	night
	spectre	strolls		sombre	
	spirit	walks			

Of your	deserted	coal-cellar		coal-cellar
	empty	hall		hall
	lonely	kitchen	and	kitchen
	solitary	living-room		living-room
	unoccupied			

And who can tell what he's	looking for
	searching for
	seeking
	trying to find

Crying				blasting	
Groaning				blowing	
Grumbling		effect		blustering	
Moaning		noise		crashing	
Screeching	with a(n)	sound	like	gale-force	wind.
Sighing		racket		noisy	
Sobbing		cacophony		sighing	
Wailing				stormy	

It can't be a ghost, you say to yourself,

Looking	over	the	window-pane
	through		window-sill

But the	world	outside is	calm		motionless
	garden		hushed		peaceful
			noiseless		serene
			peaceful	and	stationary
			placid		still
			quiet		tranquil
			silent		

	spook			
	ghost	creeps		room
The	phantom	glides	into your	bedroom
	shade	slips		bedchamber
	spectre	steals		
	spirit			

	comes			blackness
	creeps			gloom
And	slinks	up behind you in the	darkness
	sneaks			night
	steals			

		dreadful	groan
'Arrgghh!'		ghastly	grumble
'Hello'	he says with a	ghostly	moan
'Hi there,'		grisly	voice
'Whoo-oo!'		guttural	whine
		horrible	

And his voice is exactly the same as your own.

It can't be a ghost, you say to yourself

	frightened	
	nervous	
Standing there	shaking	trying to pluck
	shivering	
	trembling	

Up enough courage to turn round and look!

When you have finished compare your version with a friend's and discuss the reasons for the choices you made. Then, if you wish, you may make some changes to your own version. Finally, think of a title for the poem and make a neat copy.

Poetry Puzzle

Piece together the blotted and torn fragments of this poem. Note that because of the way the poem was torn up, and because some pieces are missing, the shape of the fragments will not give you much help in deciding their order. Work in the following way:

(1) Read the fragments and jot down their order in rough.
(2) Complete one fragment by adding a description of the 'terrifying sight'—two to six lines in length.
(3) Complete the poem by adding an ending of between ten and twenty lines.
(4) Jot down in rough the words and phrases you would use to fill in the blotted sections.
(5) Finally, write out a neat copy of the whole poem.

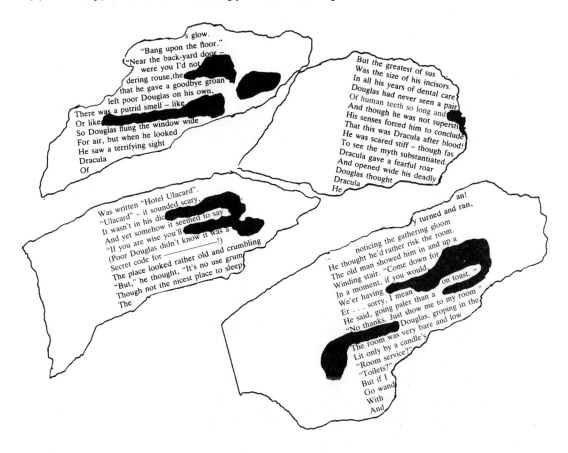

's glow."
"Bang upon the floor."
"Near the back-yard door –
were you I'd not
dering rouse, the
that he gave a goodbye groan
left poor Douglas on his own,
There was a putrid smell – like
Or like
So Douglas flung the window wide
For air, but when he looked
He saw a terrifying sight
Dracula
Of

But the greatest of sus
Was the size of his incisors.
In all his years of dental care
Douglas had never seen a pair
Of human teeth so long and
And though he was not supersti
His senses forced him to conclude
That this was Dracula after blood!
He was scared stiff – though fas
To see the myth substantiated.
Dracula gave a fearful roar
And opened wide his deadly
Douglas thought
Dracula
He

Was written "Hotel Ulacard".
"Ulacard" – it sounded scary.
It wasn't in his dic
And yet somehow it seemed to say
"If you are wise you'll
(Poor Douglas didn't know it was a
Secret code for _____!)
The place looked rather old and crumbling
"But," he thought, "It's no use grum
Though not the nicest place to sleep

an!
y turned and ran,
noticing the gathering gloom
He thought he'd rather risk the room.
The old man showed him in and up a
Winding stair. "Come down for
In a moment, if you would
We'er having   on toast."
Er . . . sorry, I mean
He said, going paler than a
"No thanks. Just show me to my room"
Douglas, groping in the
The room was very bare and low
Lit only by a candle's
"Room service?"
"Toilets?"
But if I
Go wand
With
And

18
Describe a Monster!

Imagine that you had just seen the Loch Ness monster and were trying to describe it to a friend. What would you say? Working in pairs, take it in turns to describe the monster to each other. Jot down some of the best descriptive words and phrases you thought of.

Now look at what you wrote. Many of you will have used adjectives like 'big', 'green' and 'scaly', but the best descriptions will probably be those which used some sort of comparison—'like a huge fish', 'like a large snake' or 'like a prehistoric reptile'. This kind of comparison, using the words 'like' or 'as' to compare one thing with another, is called a *simile*.

A good simile can help the reader to imagine the thing it describes. It can also influence the way you feel about the subject. For example, if you compared the Loch Ness monster to 'a huge killer whale' the reader would feel a sense of fear, but you could, if you wished, use similes which brought out the humorous side of the subject, as Ted Hughes has done in this poem:

Nessie

No, it is not an elephant or any such grasshopper.
It's shaped like a pop bottle with two huge eyes in the stopper.

But vast as a gasometer, unmanageably vast,
With sing-things like a whale for flying underwater fast.

It's me, me, me, the Monster of the Loch!
Would God I were a proper kind, a hippopot or croc!

Mislaid by the ages, I gloom here in the dark,
When I should be ruling Scotland from a throne in Regent's Park!

Once I was nobility—Diplodocus ruled the Isles!
Polyptychod came courting with his stunning ten-foot smiles.

Macroplat swore he'd carry me off before I was much older.
All his buddy-boys were by, grinning over his shoulder—

Leptoclid, Cryptocleidus, Triclid and Ichthyosteg—
Upstart Sauropterygs! But I took him down a peg—

I had a long bath in the Loch and waiting till I'd finished
He yawned himself to a fossil and his gang likewise diminished.

But now I can't come up for air without a load of trippers
Yelling: 'Look at the neck on it, and look at its hedge-clippers!

Oh no, that's its mouth.' Then I can't decently dive
Without them sighing: 'Imagine! If *that* thing were alive!

Why, we'd simply have to decamp, to Canada, and at the double!
It was luckily only a log, or the Loch-bed having a bubble.

It was something it was nothing why whatever could it be
The ballooning hideosity we thought we seemed to see?'

Because I am so ugly that it's just incredible!
The biggest bag of haggis Scotland cannot swallow or sell!

Me, me, me, the Monster of the Loch!
Scotland's ugliest daughter, seven tons of poppycock!

Living here in my black mud bed the life of a snittery newty,
And never a zoologist a-swooning for my beauty!

O where's the bonnie laddie, so bold and so free,
Will drum me up to London and proclaim my pedigree!

                                                        Ted Hughes

The Magnificent Bull

My bull is white like the silver fish in the river,
White like the shimmering crane bird on the river bank
White like fresh milk!
His roar is like thunder to the Turkish cannon on the steep shore.
My bull is dark like the raincloud in the storm.
He is like summer and winter.
Half of him is dark like the storm cloud
Half of him is light like sunshine.
His back shines like the morning star.
His brow is red like the back of the hornbill.
His forehead is like a flag, calling the people from a distance.
He resembles the rainbow.
I will water him at the river,
With my spear I shall drive my enemies.
Let them water their herds at the well;
The river belongs to me and my bull.
Drink, my bull, from the river; I am here
to guard you with my spear.

Dinka, Africa

The Thing

Its body as black as the eclipse
With yellow menacing eyes.
It stamped across the mud stricken field.
The outskirts of the town was brought alive,
Bloody carcases of horses and cattle lie.
Farmers keep watch on cattle and animals in the barn,
Shotgun at hand,
Eyes wide watching.
Morning comes,
Animal carcases scattered over the blood carpeted barn,
Broken shotgun,
No sign of farmer.
The countryside is an unsafe place.

Ian Holmes, aged 12

'Be a Monster'

I am a frightful monster,
My face is cabbage green
And even with my mouth shut
My teeth can still be seen.
My finger-nails are like rats' tails
And very far from clean.

I cannot speak a language
But make a wailing sound,
It could be any corner
You find me coming round.
Then, arms outspread and eyeballs red,
I skim across the ground.

The girls scream out and scatter
From this girl-eating bat.
I usually catch a small one
Because her legs are fat;
Or it may be she's tricked me
Wearing her grandpa's hat.

Roy Fuller

SIMILE POEMS

These poems will give you some practice in using similes. Fill in the gaps and then make up some of your own.

There's a monster in my bedroom, mum,
I'll tell you what it's like,
Its head is like

_____,

Its legs are like

_____,

Its body is like

_____,

Its claws are like

_____,

Its teeth are like

_____,

I know you don't believe me, mum,
But hurry up, it's getting closer,
It's . . . aaarrrggghhh!

A witch is like
    A dried-up old prune,
Her nose is like

_____,

Her clothes are like

_____,

Her spells are like

_____,

Her voice is like

_____,

Her manners are like

_____,

All things considered
A witch is a bit like
    My sister!

Our churchyard is like
  A set from a Hammer horror film,
The gravestones are like

——————————————,

The church is like

——————————————,

The vicar is like

——————————————,

His dog is like

——————————————,

His budgie is like

——————————————,

And every time I go there
I'm so frightened I look like

——————————————.

OTHER IDEAS FOR WRITING

Look again at your jotted descriptions of the Loch Ness monster. Add to them if you wish and then write your own poem on the subject. Describe the monster in either a terrifying or a humorous way—and choose your similes to suit.

Re-read 'The Magnificent Bull' and try to write a simile list poem in which a series of similes is used to describe one thing. This pattern may help you. Use and adapt it as freely as you like:

——————— is like ———————————
It is like ———————————,
Like ———————————,
Like ———————————,
                    etc.

Revision

Re-read Chapters Fifteen to Eighteen and then unleash all your descriptive skills on one of the titles given below. Remember above all that it is your imagination which is most important. Imagine vividly and you will write vividly, automatically using adjectives, similes, and even achieving more subtle effects which are more difficult to teach. To help you concentrate on the descriptive qualities of your poetry, it might be a good idea to write first in free verse (see Chapters One to Three), using rhyme and rhythm (see Chapters Five to Eight) as you gain confidence.

TITLES

The creature that stalks in darkness
The ogre
The mummy
The loathly worm
The THING
Lurking in the shadows . . .
The witch
Night wanderers

19
From First Draft to Final Product

Now that you have worked through this book you will find that there are so many things to consider when writing a poem that it is practically impossible to write one straight off. You have probably found already that you need to write in rough and make alterations before arriving at a final version. This process is called *drafting*, and it will help all your work (not only your poetry) if you learn to go about it in an organised way.

Even the best poets have to go through this process—in fact one of the reasons their final product is so good is that they work tremendously hard to improve their first attempts. They weigh the precise shade of meaning and sound quality of every word, making frequent alterations and improvements, sometimes taking the poem through many drafts over a period of days or months—in some cases even years! The first drafts of many famous poets still survive, and are often held in such awe that they have attracted the satirical humour of the Monty Python team. Most of the 'Famous First Drafts' from *The Brand New Monty Python Bok* are too rude to print here, but here is one of the milder examples:

Ode to a ~~Gynaecologist~~ ~~Barmau~~ ~~Nightwatchman~~ ingale

My heart goes ~~ping!~~ aches

And a ~~lousy~~ drowsy numbness pains my sense

As though of ~~Watneys~~ Hemlock I had drunk

Or ~~thrown up all over your carpet~~ emptied some dull opiate to the drains

Alright, officer ~~I'll come quietly~~

This is a real example, complete with sketch, from Spike Milligan:

Terence Newt
Wore a Giant boot
Jammed down over his head
And he kept it there
~~With some of care~~ {with his ears and Craw}
Until the day he was dead.
But when his wife removed the Boot,
She discovered to her Horror!
It was not the Head of Terence Newt
But three other men. Tom Daft an apprentice
butcher, Cyril hunge a Mechanic and Arthur Woggs. Dentist.

114

DRAFTING YOUR OWN WORK

Begin by jotting down your ideas, along with suitable words, phrases and rhymes, as they come to you.

Assemble these jottings into a first draft of the poem.

Read it through carefully, checking the following points:

General: Is there anything that you have not described clearly? Is there anything that doesn't make sense? Are there any unnecessary words, phrases or lines? Cross them out. Can the layout of lines and verses be improved?

Repetition: Are there any places where you could effectively repeat words or phrases? Has the poem a satisfying ending? If not, try repeating the opening lines, or one or two of the best lines at the end (see Chapters One to Three).

Rhyme: Remember the golden rules:

Rhymes must sound perfectly natural—*never* use an unsuitable word just because it rhymes.
Rhymes shouldn't lead you to say something you didn't intend to say.

Rhythm: Does the rhythm of your poem flow smoothly without any awkward halts or jerks? If you can't get the rhythm to sound right, count up the syllables and mark in the stresses (see Chapters Six and Seven). This may show you where you went wrong.

Alliteration: Are there any places where you could have used alliteration to good effect? (See Chapters Ten and Eleven.)

Description: Can any of your describing words be changed for ones which are more vivid? Consult the list which you made when working through Chapter Sixteen.

Synonyms: Have you tried to find the word which has exactly the right shade of meaning for what you want to say? (See Chapter Seventeen.)

Similes: Have you used similes to help the reader imagine your subject? Are they effective? (See Chapter Eighteen.)

Finally: Check for correct English. Are the spellings correct? Does the punctuation (if any) help to make the meaning clear? Have you used capital letters where necessary?

When you have considered all these points write out a second draft. At this stage it will be useful to discuss it with a friend, or with the teacher—they will bring a fresh viewpoint to your problems.

The final product will depend on what you or your teacher wants to do with your poem. Most often it will simply be a neat copy of the final draft, but occasionally it may be printed in a school or class poetry magazine, or be presented as part of a wall display. These will require a special effort at presentation. If you have any artistic talent you could design a decorative border, or draw an illustration to go with your poem. These examples by poets and pupils will give you some ideas:

Anna Mason, aged 11

The Undead

By Barry Brooks YI

He comes to haunt ye!
Hobbling through the graveyard,
While from his path a hare
Flees like a shadow. On he comes,
Through the forest dark where a wolf howls ~
No soaring lark did ever sing here.

Dark sinister clouds obscure the moon,
The fog creeps up on you like the tide
Devouring land as it goes
The stench of death following in its path.
From the earth a groping hand appears,
Nails like razors, skin like a toad,
Warty and grotesque, tearing at the earth.
Revealing the undead!

Pale flashes rise in his eyes
As he sees before him a maiden fair
And holds her in his gaze.
Her heart beats wildly at the sight
But no move can she make
His cruel spell to break.

O HERE IT IS AND
THERE IT IS ...

Mervyn Peake.

O here it is! and there it is!
And no-one knows whose share it is!
Nor dares to stake a claim—
But we have seen it in the air,
A fairy, like a William pear—
With but itself to blame.

A thug it is! and smug it is;
And like a floating pug it is,
Above the orchard trees.
It has no right—no right at all
To soar above the orchard wall
With chilblains on its knees.

The SICK ROSE

O Rose thou art sick.
The invisible worm.
That flies in the night
In the howling storm:

Has found out thy bed
Of crimson joy:
And his dark secret love
Does thy life destroy.

William Blake

Poetry Puzzle

Refresh your memory of Chapters Fifteen to Nineteen and then try to improve this dull and lifeless first draft of a horror poem by replacing some of the words and phrases with more exciting ones. Use as much freedom as necessary to bring the poem to life. Change the descriptive words for more vivid ones, trying to get exactly the shade of meaning you want, build up the atmosphere of the poem, and make the similes more appropriate and effective. Add appropriate punctuation to your final draft.

The wood was very dark
And full of dark shadows
The full moon was very bright
Like a plate in the sky

Then I heard a strange noise
Like the screeching of a rusty gate
And when I looked I saw a strange shape
Hiding in the bushes

So I ran away very quickly
But it could run more quickly
And it got nearer and nearer
I felt very frightened

I turned round to look
It was a large and ugly wolf-man
His ugly mouth was open wide
And his teeth were like a row of bread-knives

A. M. Oron

20
Your Poetic Licence

Now that you have come to the end of this book, you have well and truly earned your poetic licence! Congratulations! But remember that getting a licence is more of a beginning than an end. If you had just obtained your driving licence you would be looking forward to a lifetime of driving—and now that you have got your poetic licence you should continue to read and write poetry!

Well done! You've read this book,
Shivered at shadows and shook
At wizened witch and wizard,
Gruesome ghoul and spook!

Talking, acting, laughing,
Reading, drawing, writing:
Not bad at all for school!
Surprisingly exciting!

You've also learned a lot
And didn't even know it,
You've got your licence too,
And now you are a poet!

Chris Webster

Poetic Licence
THIS IS TO CERTIFY THAT

- -

has worked through this tome and in so doing has written ____ poems, consulted dictionaries & thesaurusi, solved ____ poems, ached with laughter and suffered numerous nightmares.

He/She is now a **POET**, and is entitled to the following freedoms:

- to do without punctuation or capital letters
- to alter the usual order of words ✓ to alter spelling
- to vary the rhythm or rhyme scheme as required
- to invent verse forms and rhyme schemes
- to invent words (BUT ONLY IN POETRY!)

He/She is licenced for a lifetime of Poetic Pleasure which begins today:

date _ _ _ _ _ _ _ _

signed _ _ _ _ _ _ _ _ _ _ (Class Teacher)

signed _ _ _ _ _ _ _ _